Believe In
NOTHING
& Set Yourself Free

How To
Believe In
NOTHING
& Set Yourself Free

Michael Misita

Printed in the United States of America.
First Printing: July 1994
Valley of the Sun Publishing, Box 38, Malibu, CA 90265

ISBN: 0-87554-572-6
Library of Congress Card Number: 94-060391

DEDICATION

To my friend Alzada ...
and to all those who have nurtured me.

ACKNOWLEDGEMENTS

"Originality," it has been said, "is merely unconscious plagiarism." The ideas shared in this book are not new, but it is my hope that I have brought them a bit closer to the readers' understanding of their practicality in everyday life. My heartfelt thanks to all the wonderful writers and teachers who have greatly influenced my life and these writings—especially J. Krishnamurti, Bhagwan Shree Rajneesh and Sri Nisargadatta. If I have inadvertantly quoted or paraphrased from any source without crediting them, it was unintentional. I give thanks to all, both physical and non-physical.

The reader should note: Any use of the word "man" in this text is generic and denotes a person of either sex.

Special Acknowledgements: Richard and Tara Sutphen for their encouragement, enthusiasm and confidence in my work; Sharon Boyd, Jason McKean, Jim Hagopian and Irene French Harvey for their artistic talents.

My love to "The Weezer," Bob, Michael, Betty, Sandy, Jim, Jeff, Robert, and Carolyn.

CONTENTS

CONTENTS

1

HOW TO BELIEVE IN NOTHING

*"I believe in everything ...
and I believe in nothing."*

"Beliefs are part of our struggle **not** to be free. I believe in everything and I believe in nothing." When people hear me say that in my lectures, I usually get a few puzzled looks until I explain there is no contradiction in that statement. There is room for the total spectrum of possibilities in the universe. To believe in something is always limiting; believing in nothing is non-specific. There is freedom from limitation because there are no particulars.

At this point, someone says, "But, *everybody* has to believe in *something*. I believe in this ideology (or that person, place or thing) and it freed me." Maybe it did ... temporarily.

The possibility of living without the need to believe is very threatening to many people. In a world of uncertainty, the loss of something to hold on to can be frightening. I understand that. I am not saying that you **must** believe in nothing—if your beliefs work for you, that's fine. There is absolutely nothing wrong with believing in anything. The desire to believe is built into the human mind, which is constructed to make judgments and form opinions. Without this ability to be critical and discerning, the human race would not have survived very long. It is when these judgments and opinions become dogmatic that they are no longer life-enhancing but limiting. If your beliefs don't work for you, you need to take another look at them. Your beliefs may be blocking you from being as happy or as fulfilled as you would like to be.

To suggest that people consider dropping even one of their beliefs, especially beliefs about God, makes them extremely uncomfortable. I merely encourage people to see and understand the accumulations and boundaries they have and how they are creating and sustaining them. I'm suggesting that those who wish to be more aware, more awake—those who want to be free—begin by investigating their beliefs, especially the belief that you need your beliefs.

I have worked with many people who experience limitation in their lives because they believe in limitation, and I've helped them to expand their consciousness by encouraging them to believe in prosperity. Others say they don't believe in themselves, but it's not belief they lack, it's self-confidence. There are a lot of books and other materials available to help people reprogram their mind with new beliefs. Replacing negative mental programming with positive programming can help them live happier, more satisfying lives. There's nothing wrong with that.

In my own life, I have studied the internal workings of my mind and experienced the power of thought by encountering my illusions first-hand. As all that I persisted in believing manifested itself in my world, I became increasingly aware of the power of belief and its potent effect. I began to observe what I believed to be true about myself and the world around me. When I discovered that much of my reality was shaped by my beliefs *about* what was real rather than by reality itself, I began to question not only what I believed, but why I needed those beliefs. Suddenly, I felt stripped of all my ideas about reality—those giving me pleasure as well as those I thought gave my life stability. I began to understand the extent of and the reason for my psychological bondage.

How do we handle the confusion we feel when we move to the level of consciousness where we cease exchanging one belief in favor of another and begin to question belief itself? What is the nature of our existence when we begin to see that our illusions are illusions? This is what this book is about—the transcendence of belief to the fullness of being.

You won't find a new set of beliefs to replace your old ones; instead, you'll discover a new way of looking at everything you encounter. I'll share my experiences and those of others who have learned to transcend their beliefs and set themselves free, as well as techniques you can use to do the same. Instead of reacting with preconceived ideas and conditioned responses, you'll move into a new state of consciousness that will be infinitely more insightful, freeing and rewarding than anything you've known before.

On a personal level, I have found this to be true. In sharing what I've experienced, I do my part in helping people to know themselves a little better, to begin to know themselves as the source of their own misery. Also, my conscious awareness deepens within me as a by-product of sharing. I don't do what I do for a reason. These are just observations of what happens as a result of sharing. To the common mind, this may appear to be a motive, but being oneself is completely beyond all motivation. You can't have a reason for being yourself. You are yourself, and no reason is needed. Whether or not anyone actually acts on what I'm sharing is irrelevant to me. I can only share from where I am right now and only with those who show an interest.

Without understanding that we carry the seeds of our potential, there is no possibility for transformation; but if we are fortunate enough to have a glimpse of those possibilities, we will summon the courage to make the necessary effort to bring about our own transformation, whatever the cost. In doing so, we will discover that it has been well worth it.

This book is not for people who need to believe in something, it is for people who are at the level where they are ready to stop conditioning altogether. They are becoming more and more present. They are ready for the next step, which is to question not just their various belief systems but why they believe at all. This will propel them into a space beyond the ordinary herd mentality. It's a jump ... a leap ... into the unknown.

Until you take this leap, all beliefs will create a burden. They will not liberate you. If you can be open enough to realize whatever you believe in is limited and that reality—the truth—is limitless, you'll discover something of which ninety-nine percent of the world is unaware ... freedom from belief.

2

WHAT ARE BELIEFS?

"Your experiences in life are conditioned by your beliefs, so they are never totally accurate. You must take this into account, but you must also begin somewhere."

What are beliefs, then? Belief can be described as any interpretation or framework for viewing reality that is held beyond questioning. The word "belief" comes from the Old English word *geliefan*, which comes from the Indo-European base *leubh*, which is related to the Latin word *libido*, meaning "what is desired, or loved."

From the very roots of the word, we see what beliefs truly are—that which we desire to be so. Because beliefs are a construct of the mind, freedom from them allows the individual to begin to experience the aliveness of his total being.

Beliefs are ideas that we have either made up or that have been passed on to us. They are concepts that we have not acquired through our own experience. Belief conditions experience and experience then strengthens belief. What you believe, you experience. The mind is a result of its experience; it can recognize only that which is familiar. Experience is not necessarily reality. Desire conditions the mind, and belief is another cloak of desire. You want what you want to be true. Knowledge, belief, conviction, and conclusion are hindrances to truth. Belief in a Master creates the Master. Belief in a dogma or a specific design of action does produce what is longed for, but for a price. If a person has the potential, belief can become a weapon more dangerous than any gun. For most of us, belief has more significance than actuality. To understand *what is*, you don't need belief; on the contrary, beliefs prejudice one's understanding. But beliefs warm and comfort us. Belief produces a feeling of power and can be subtly seductive.

If you know something to be true, it is no longer a belief, it is a fact. Beliefs are not facts. There is a vast difference between a fact and the idea of a fact. A belief is an idea of what we hope to be a fact, but it is an idea that is based on possibility, not actuality. We may fervently desire it to be the truth, but it is not the truth. Understanding a fact does not necessarily bring joy. Understanding a fact may cause a disturbance in you, and what you want is comfort. Beliefs are often used to gain status. The ego is strengthened as a result of feeling its particular beliefs to be the truth. Individuals and groups hope to gain an advantage by wielding power over other individuals and groups. "I (we) know the truth and you don't. Therefore, I am right and you are wrong." This must be seen for what it is: the ego's game. But truth gives no power over others. Truth cannot be harnessed by the ego for a purpose of any kind. It must be wanted for its own sake.

Rigid mental frameworks make it difficult to entertain any new idea, let alone accept it. In fact, most people will accept a new point of view only if it conforms in some way to their current beliefs and does not take them beyond the limited view of their own horizons.

So, beliefs are a way of limiting ourselves. They are the mental limits we place on ourselves ... and those limits can be stronger than any chains ever made. People accumulate beliefs throughout their lives. Some we grew up with, others are added by the people we associate with. They're comfortable. The last thing most people would ever want is to question their beliefs. Instead, they look for others to reinforce their beliefs because they think the more people who believe in something, the truer that thing becomes. Needing verification of their beliefs, people are attracted to other people and groups who think as they do. The search is to find this verification, not to find anything new which may disturb them. The search for truth is usually the search for proof of what is already believed to be true, not what is true.

This is particularly evident with religious and spiritually minded people and ideas. Take Galileo, for example. The majority of the world's population believed the earth was flat, and became enraged when he offered scientific proofs that it was round. The Catholic Church persecuted him for not believing the earth was flat. It was only a few years ago that the Church officially agreed Galileo was right.

But if a person is free of those beliefs, they can go anywhere—to any church, any group—and be perfectly happy and content because nothing need upset them. It is incredibly freeing when you can go anywhere, be with any type of person and feel complete in yourself. You don't need to have anyone verify your beliefs, and you become a more interesting person, more alive, free to come and go as you will. You're open to new ideas and are able to act appropriately in any situation—you know what to do, what to say, how to act. You act purely without the need for motive.

Why? Because you're free of restricting ideas and beliefs

about the situation. You don't have preconceived ideas, or at least you're able to see that they are preconceived ideas. You can say to somebody, "Well I believe this or that," and know that it's actually a belief that you have. You don't have to fight for your belief or debate whether it's true or not.

IDEAS AND PERCEPTIONS

In his essay, "Summa Theologica," Thomas Aquinas discusses the process by which ideas are formed: "We remember past events or happenings but we are never aware of the memories by which we remember them. We can be aware of imagined or imaginary objects but never the images by which we imagine them. We apprehend objects of thought but never the concepts by which we think of them."

Human beings are complex, not simple. For example, they think but they also feel. The relationship of thinking and feeling is interactional and cyclical. The way we structure our world makes us feel about it in certain ways. The way we feel affects what we pay attention to and how we make sense of it.

When we look at the world through these impressions, we are enclosed and biased by those images. Because all that we see and hear must be filtered through the concepts that we hold of ourselves and the world around us, we never really see anything around us with an objective eye. For instance, each person is different at every moment and so are we, but the mind is in the habit of looking with the perceptions it has previously formed and those perceptions may have nothing whatever to do with who or what that person or thing is right now. I'm sure everyone has had the experience of meeting an old friend not seen for years and being disappointed that the person is not the person he knew before.

People usually reach a conclusion based on a single observation—a fragment of the picture—and then magnify that grain of truth until it is completely out of proportion. A waiter treats you poorly and you hate waiters. A man treats you badly and you hate all men. You don't like Saddam Hussein, so you mistrust all Iraqis. There is a great tendency to embrace myths and fantasies because we want to, although life is not nearly as complicated as we make it out to be.

My observation is that we don't know what we are doing or why, or even why we are here. The mind only makes up ideas to pacify us, and we fall for them. When your mind hears a statement like "You can be free of your beliefs," the mind will start calling everything a belief because it wants to continue to assert its influence. Your mind doesn't want you to know there is a knowing beyond beliefs where the mind's influence ceases.

Most people lead a life of lies and false conclusions, clinging desperately to their beliefs. Frequently, when people realize that what they believe may not be true, they will do a flip-flop and embrace the reverse of what they had previously believed. A group I was asked to facilitate illustrates this observation very well.

The intense anger generated by the circle of people was almost overwhelming. I resisted the urge to flee as I surveyed the group comprised of people recently disenchanted with religious and spiritual organizations they had believed in for years. Hostility and disappointment were evident on every face. Some had signed over homes and property to these groups; others had given their time, money, and services, and now felt victimized. They felt they had been betrayed, so they gathered with other people—who believed as they did—to form a group whose purpose, it seemed to me, was revenge.

One of the angriest people in the group was a middle-aged man who once had been a devout believer in his church's doctrines for more than fourteen years. Now he said he was an atheist. What he had done was to replace one set of beliefs with another set, going from one extreme to the other. This was the only way he could redirect the energy that was freed when he released his old beliefs. The all-encompassing, energy-consuming belief system left a void that he replaced with something equally encompassing and energy-consuming—rage, resentment and indignation. His ego, acting on his belief that he had been taken advantage of, projected any responsibility for his own actions onto his former church, which he then completely discredited.

I suggested that he could learn from the experience, if he would look at the more positive side. I asked him what he had learned, pointing out that he had obviously gained from the experience, having had some wonderful times belonging to the church as long as he had. I also told him there is always a degree of truth to be found in every group, but no matter how I tried to help him see the situation clearly, he as fervently espoused atheism as he had his former belief system. He could not see that he essentially hadn't changed a thing. Instead of acknowledging his hurt and the loss of his beliefs and allowing that energy to move him into a period of not knowing, his mind quickly replaced one false sense of knowing with another. He still wasn't free.

This is only counterbalancing within a limited dimension. The addiction to the idea of duality needs to be released. To transcend to a higher dimension, the negative or positive nature of any belief is irrelevant.

Why would you want to hang on to something that isn't true? Because you don't know or don't want to know what *is* true. So you replace the insecure feeling of not knowing with an idea that gives you the satisfying feeling that you do know. However, truth is never a conclusion; it is always a realization, a revelation.

Sometimes you will hold onto a belief that causes you pain, even though you know your belief is unreasonable. The pain may be all you have to cling to, and it is not readily relinquished even though you may say that you want to release it.

A friend named Clara was experiencing severe distress over her mother's death, even though the woman had died many years before. She was unable to face her feelings of guilt over not being with her mother while she was ill, so she blamed the nurses, the hospital, her brother and his wife, the doctors, and God—in short, she concluded that everyone and everything else was to blame for not taking care of her mother properly. If she let go of the blame she directed at others, she would be forced to deal with her unvoiced belief that she was to blame. No amount of reasoning or understanding would convince her to accept other than what she wanted to believe, even though she claimed she wanted to stop her grief and loneliness. Seeing that she needed to hold onto those beliefs, I let her go.

Six months later, Clara showed up at my door, a completely changed person. She radiated happiness and contentment. I asked her what had happened to relieve her distress and she told me that what I had said to her about observing herself had finally penetrated her mind. In her loneliness and despair, she had finally hit bottom and turned to the only person left who would pay attention to her—herself. She had taken an honest, clear look at herself and her situation from a detached perspective and was able to accept responsibility for her role in creating the situation. She let go of the need to blame either herself or anyone else. This released enough energy to bring about change and allowed her the freedom to get on with her own life.

When we begin to observe, we start becoming aware of our conclusions. If we have already decided something is wrong or right, we cannot watch. The mind is a very subtle thing. Whatever you see, you see through the mind; whatever you listen to, you listen to through the mind—and the mind is quick at imposing interpretations.

WHAT CAN WE REALLY KNOW ABOUT ANYTHING?

You may think that your beliefs define who you are; that's not true. Who you *really* are has nothing to do with what you believe. Your beliefs only define the limitations your mind places on your character and personality. It's like being an actor. The actor is not the character he portrays on the stage, no matter how convincing the performance. Sir Laurence Olivier was not Hamlet or King Lear; he merely portrayed these personalities. In real life, Sylvester Stallone is neither Rocky nor Rambo.

In the same way, beliefs are the patterns through which we play out our parts in the world. When you begin to see through the belief systems you've been using to define the character you're playing in this world, that character begins to dissolve and the actor himself begins to show up.

To release belief, it is necessary to become fully aware of the psychological interplay between belief (in the part you're playing) and the self (the real actor). Then you are able to see the falsehood behind belief.

When you begin to see this within yourself, you will become aware that those around you—family, friends, lovers, neighbors, co-workers, etc.—are also actors playing roles of limitation. The difference is that they aren't aware they're playing roles. You begin to understand, and in understanding, there is no need to stay angry, to condemn or criticize ... or to forgive. Understand yourself first, and you will understand the world around you.

Through the years I've worked with hundreds of people who have problems with their parents. They complain that their parents don't accept them for who or what they are. "You can't expect a turtle to run like a deer," I tell them. I point out that they want unconditional acceptance from their parents but are unwilling to unconditionally accept their parents. The problem lies within themselves; their parents are simply the scapegoats. A person who wants to be truly free must refuse to place limits on others as well as refusing to accept limitations from others.

Freeing yourself is not about hindsight. It's about being aware of what you are doing, saying and feeling *as it occurs*. Let's say you've gotten angry about something, and you decide to talk it over with your therapist at the next session. By then it will be too late. The anger experience is over and you'll have had many other experiences in the meantime. Just talking won't help much—you've got to be aware of it at the very moment it occurs. Once the moment is over, it's too late. Conjuring up the experience won't help much either, because it was yesterday's anger, yesterday's energy, and it is lost forever. It's easy to be reasonable after the fact. "Oh, I'll never do that again!" Yes, you will, and you'll continue doing so until you catch yourself in the act. I'm not saying it does no good to let out your emotions and have catharsis, but these techniques are limited. They help somewhat, but they don't free you because they only deal with the past, not the present. You must be alert when similar energy arises in you again and experience the energy *as it is happening*, with full awareness.

To release belief, it is necessary to become fully aware of the psychological interplay between belief and self; when you are able to see the falsehood behind belief, the habit will vanish.

At this point, you attain the intuitive insight that comes from recognizing and acknowledging the limitations of the mind. You shed the false protection of belief and allow yourself to operate within what I call "the security of insecurity." You begin to see beliefs as merely conditioned ways of knowing and applying knowledge that is relative, not absolute.

Since I've been using acting as an example, I'll use it again to further explain what I mean. I was a professional actor most of my life. Actors are very insecure people. Every actor knows that acting is not the field a person who wants stability or financial security should be in, yet we find ourselves drawn to that lifestyle. The Screen Actors Guild, a union for actors, estimates that only about five percent of the thousands of actors in the union actually make their living by acting. If you've ever been around actors, the most common topic of discussion is how miserable they are that they are not working and how uncertain they always feel. Years ago, I realized that, as an actor, sometimes I would work, and most of the time I probably would not work. I accepted the inherent instability of this profession, and in doing so, I found stability. I never tried to be secure in the field, nor did I permit acting to dictate whether or not I was happy. This was the security of insecurity.

Acceptance is the key here. The world is like this. Accept it as it is, and you are free of it. Accept your parents for who they are and you are free of them. What makes you miserable is your desire to have things and people be other than what they are. You want a turtle to run like a deer and you want a lion to be like a sheep. Look deeply, and you will see that the only time you are angry and unhappy is when things are not as you want them to be. When you believe in particulars, you cause your own pain. Let go of the particulars, and you will flow freely.

What can we expect of life when we are emancipated from our belief systems? In that liberation lies the pathless domain of freedom—the beginning of discovery. By realizing and accepting that we live in a world of insecurity, we are then moved into a place of peace that does not rely on external conditions.

3
WHY WE BELIEVE

*"If the thing believed is
incredible, it is also incredible
that the incredible should
have been so believed."*

SAINT AUGUSTINE

Beliefs are part of your struggle **not** to be free. You cling to the false because you do not know the true. Your mind doesn't want you to know there is a knowing beyond beliefs where the mind's influence ceases.

If you think your beliefs give you peace of mind, be aware that beliefs are lazy things—they replace what is real. Don't make the mistake of thinking a lazy mind is a peaceful mind. A lazy mind can't be bothered to find out the truth of a situation or thing because it requires too much effort. Preconceived ideas produce a lazy mind. You've already decided the way a person is or how a situation will be. There is no room to explore, which limits your experiences. It requires alertness to keep the mind clear and maturity to live life in the full awareness of every moment as it happens, no matter what the cost. The fear is that the ego may be shattered and only a spiritually mature person has the courage to allow that to happen. But if a person wishes to grow, living life in the present, which may at times seem painful and tragic, is the most important thing because the present is the only door to reality. Once through it, you will then begin to see the lack of value in what you have been holding onto.

Why is it so difficult to remain in the present? You get frightened and you get bored. You're looking for something to turn you on, to get you moving, but at the same time you're afraid to end your boredom. You want the real to be what you want it to be ... not what it is. It's an awful block. I often refer to it as the "Great Barrier." But it is possible to be free if you'll allow yourself to see clearly and you can only see clearly if you see beyond the images, the beliefs that are blocking the view.

People protest that their beliefs are true, but people are hungry to have experiences, especially spiritual experiences. They don't realize that it is relatively easy to conjure an experience out of their belief system, but that experience is more fantasy than real. Real "mystical" experiences must come unaided. The less you are involved in producing them, the more genuine they are. Then they must be released immediately or they will self-create more of the same. Mystical experiences are intoxicating and there lies the danger in them for those who wish to become more aware.

All beliefs contain an element of truth that gives the whole belief the feeling of being true. Your beliefs wouldn't exist without your believing *in* them. Are you more interested in *your* truth, in being right, or in truth itself? Truth stands alone; it doesn't need *your* belief to give it reality.

Truth is one, it cannot be divided. It has no ownership and does not need to be defended. Are you more interested in what you *think* is real or in discovering what *is* real? A belief may be ninety-nine percent false and only one percent true. It's ridiculous to base one's whole life on that ratio without ever examining it.

Beliefs frequently masquerade as fact. Though they sometimes have a useful function in making sense of our experience of the physical world, when they discourage scrutiny instead of challenging us to further thought, we need to examine the belief until we see the false percentage in it. *When you let that false percentage go, what's left will be one hundred percent true, and you won't need to maintain the belief any more.*

ADDICTIVE STATES

Belief is a habit—a habit with intellectual content. It is also an addiction. You may not have thought of yourself as a belief junkie, but your beliefs shackle you as much as any heroin addict's needle. Addiction can be defined as an individual's adjustment to his environment, an habitual style of coping that has compulsive qualities.

Eddie couldn't drink just one cup of coffee; he had to drink twenty. He was also a recovering alcoholic. He approached belief systems in the same way. Eric Hoffer coined the phrase "true believer" to describe such a person. When Eddie first came to the gathering, he was afraid of his feelings and avoided them by being very intellectual. He wanted everything to be clearly and sharply defined. He also wanted to be in control of any situation he encountered, but from the moment he arrived, he was dealing with the unexpected. I continued to keep him off-balance.

I felt he would be helped by the realization that he might not know as much as he thought he did. After he would make a statement in the group, I would remind him that what he had just said was probably a belief or theory, and he really didn't know for sure the validity of what he was saying. I used this tactic to open up a mind rigidly set on having all the answers. He became able to say "I really know nothing," and mean it. This freed him and enabled him to consider other possibilities. He was also able to explore his feelings and be less guarded.

My tactic had worked, almost too well. When it was time for him to release the idea that he didn't know anything, his addictive personality was unable to let go. He would say, "I don't know" all the time to the point where it not only was annoying to have a conversation with him, but it became a block to his further growth. On numerous occasions, I told him he had now made an addiction out of this statement, that it had become a habit, thereby losing its value for him. It took a while—he had to be weaned off the statement the same way he had weaned himself off coffee and alcohol, but he eventually moved past it.

Be aware of statements like this that have become habitual detriments to your growth.

Look at the beliefs people have about their relationships. I work with many people who have problems with relationships. In fact, **every** problem is a relationship problem—how you relate to money, success, happiness, sex, the universe, and so on.

When Freda came to me, she had just been divorced and was about to marry her seventh husband. As we talked about her relationship issues, she told me how rotten her previous husbands had been, how they had mistreated her and how screwed up they were. Then she said something really interesting. "Now I'm on to another one."

I tried to show her how her belief system about marriage kept her in a cycle, attracting the same kind of person over and over again, but she denied it. She wouldn't see that she was in any way responsible. She continued to complain about her bad relationships with men until I was so exasperated, I said, "You know, I'm trying to get you to focus on the positive side of it, but you just keep telling me the same stories over and over again."

Freda hesitated for a second, then said, "I know, but I just love talking about it."

I told her, "Your next husband isn't going to be any different. You'll have the same problems with him because you believe all men are the same—rotten, miserable wife abusers, and you can't trust them. You'll produce the same situation again because that's what you believe in, only each time it will become more intolerable until you 'get it.' You're addicted to that belief."

Everything possible to believe has this potential to become addictive. We either cling to a particular belief, even though it may have outgrown its temporary usefulness, or replace it with another. We replace the idea of lack with the idea of prosperity, the idea of hatred with the idea of love, and so on. The habituation of our beliefs is a good indication that we have probably stopped learning. If we believe that we already know, we will not be able to observe and experience the freshness of life. Recognizing that we actually don't know moves us into the present moment. Then, suddenly, things begin to happen. A crossover occurs and we move into the unexpected, into the aliveness of life. We become available to the new.

DESIRE

Ever transient and insatiable, desire is the pursuit of

illusion; its purpose is to give the mind a sense of security. We find the reality of who we *believe* ourselves to be unsatisfying. Out of this constant, disturbing dissatisfaction arises fear, which we identify as either physically or psychologically painful. Consequently, we want to become other than what we are. Quick-fix fads and bandaid solutions such as those featured in supermarket tabloids and popular magazines appeal to these desires, promising the moon but delivering only its reflection. We will go to any length to avoid seeing what *is*; as a result, our decisions are motivated by the desire for pleasure and the fear of pain. We don't understand what we are now so we avoid facing it by creating something else. We lull ourselves to sleep with our beliefs, our rituals, our food, drink, sex and ideals—all diversions to avoid being disturbed. Disturbance is not a bad thing—it's necessary for anyone who wishes to grow because only then do we question. Without disturbance, there is stagnation. Observe the ebb and flow of water in the ocean or a river or stream—the disturbance keeps the water fresh and alive. Look along the edges where the water isn't in motion—the vitality has left, causing the water to stagnate.

As we look deeper, we see that desire pushes us forward and our old companion, fear, holds us back. We understand the language of fear, the origin of which we have forgotten until we begin to observe ourselves, for when fear speaks to us, we obey.

We want meaningful relationships but panic at even the hint of a commitment; we desire success but are anxious about it; we want to be happy but feel undeserving; we hunger for recognition but worry that we are incapable of living up to our religious or social ideals. It's one great big tug-of-war.

What makes us afraid is that we reject what we innately know to be the *actual* while clinging to the *illusion*. We are terrified of being insecure, both physically and psychologically, and of not achieving our desires, either for ourselves or another. Our real motive is to be safe and protected. However, in an insecure world, the fulfillment of pleasure is dubious at best.

Can we look at our world as it is, without trying to escape from the truth? Can we face our aloneness, our fears, our relationships, our insecurities about the world, without resorting to distractions? Can we observe ourselves without comparisons, judgments, condemnations?

The real issue is, can you not recondition yourself? That's the question. Can you not go from one side to the other, but transcend both sides and go beyond both sides? In other words, go beyond all conditioning. You see, it's not just a matter of questioning your beliefs, although that's how it starts. Once you start investigating what you believe in, eventually the real question is not why do I believe in these things, but why do I believe at all? You begin to question belief itself. Why do we believe? What is the necessity behind belief? Why do I need to believe?

Consciousness is not pure awareness but rather awareness as it is embodied in the psychological structure of the mind or the brain. Awareness exists independently of the brain structure. At the point when you start questioning belief, you will begin to move into a different state of consciousness, then transcend consciousness to awareness. You will move beyond all this talk of love and hate, of being this or that. The content of consciousness will cease to be the yardstick by which you measure your life because it is based on a limited sense of identity. Awareness will become more and more important. The very act of seeing the complexity of the web you've woven around yourself is all that's required for the whole structure to collapse all at once, and you'll be in a state of freedom which you've never experienced before. That is the nature of observing.

Judgment separates and divides by deciding in what class or category an act belongs. It compares, distributes, estimates but creates nothing. It cannot originate ideas because it is of the past. Transformation requires the deep acceptance of our being as we are now, without judgment.

THE HEART OF THE MATTER

Why are we so ambitious? Why do we continually seek to make the "I" amount to something? "I have to be good, I have to be right, I have to be loving, successful, heroic, modest, spiritual, etc." Why are we so concerned with the future and the past?

Honesty is a rarity where motives are concerned because it takes enormous energy and courage to look at ourselves. We may find it too disturbing to see the genuine motives behind our actions, so we cleverly conceal them behind a multitude of masks: humility, generosity, virtue, respectability, to name a few. Revealing the truth behind these masks, we fear, might thwart the gratification of our ambitions. We want to be successful to glorify our beliefs, our ideals, or ourselves; this only serves to widen the gap separating us from each other.

First we have a motive, out of which arise our inclinations, which may be considered good or bad, ethical or unethical, moral or immoral. If we each look deeply within ourselves to find out where our pleasures lie, our inclinations are revealed to us. We can then discern whether these inclinations come from our inherited (genetic) mechanism or from our acquired concepts (which come from our environment and are also mechanical) or both. A closer look at the reason for our choices reveals the heart of the matter, which is that our beliefs are produced in our world according to our motives.

Giving and getting are not based on what we think we do but on the motive behind our actions. That motive is always based on achieving pleasure and avoiding pain. Dr. J.C. Arthur, in his book entitled *The Sagacity and Morality of Plants,* says: "I have tried to show that all organisms, even to the very simplest, whether plant or animal, from the very nature of life and the struggle for its maintenance, must be endowed with conscious feeling—pleasure and pain being its simplest expression."

Years ago, when I first started speaking, I began receiving gifts from people attending the groups I held. At first I was flattered. I thought of the gifts as being given freely, with no strings attached, but after a while I realized some of them were bribes, not gifts. What is the difference between a gift and a bribe? The dictionary defines a gift as "given or bestowed without charge. The action, right, or power of giving." Bribery is defined as "something to induce a certain course of action, especially a wrong course by the gift or offer of something valued." Most of what we do in life is motivated by our desire to "get." Rarely, if ever, do we give freely to another or ourselves. Bribery is very subtle and cunning, and often disguises itself as good intent.

I remember going with a friend to see a famous teacher from India one evening. I was asked to bring a piece of fruit as an offering to the guru as it was considered a symbolic gesture of giving in return for the wisdom we were about to receive. When we got there, the room was filled with over a thousand devotees. After the talk and meditation, a long line formed as we waited patiently to present our small tokens of gratitude. In front of me was a man whose arms were full of dolls, posters, a basket of fruit and other things. The single apple I held suddenly seemed inadequate.

When the man's turn came, several attendants came forward to help him lay his gifts on the floor before the teacher. The crowd murmured its appreciation of this impressive offering while waiting to see the guru's response. The teacher took one look at the items presented to him and waved the man away, refusing his gifts with a flick of the hand. The man protested that the presents were for him but again the guru waved the man away and told his attendants to return the presents to the man. The attendants escorted the man from the hall.

As we milled around afterward, I overheard some of the people in the crowd criticizing the guru, saying that his actions were not very loving. I realized that it was the man's motives that were in question here. The teacher would not accept these gifts because he recognized them as a bribe for attention that would enhance the man's ego, therefore the teacher immediately refused the presents and dismissed the man.

When a person wants something in life, whether it be an object, a relationship, success, money, or awareness, he must question his real motive for wanting these things. He must be as honest with himself as possible. If he finds he wants these things for questionable reasons, then he must face this honestly if he is to ever grow in awareness.

IMAGINATION AND CHOICE

Paul was a difficult person to speak with. He had been raised in the kind of insecurity only a broken home could produce, and had a mind-set that was rigidly unyielding. He had recently attended several large metaphysical seminars where he was told "You are unlimited. You can do anything." He believed that his life had changed for the better as a result of these affirmations. His first taste of personal power completely seduced him.

Many metaphysically inclined people have the idea that thought as expressed in imagination or creative visualization is the ultimate expression of self, yet this idea shackles them because thought, as expressed in the human form, is limited by experience of the senses. Individuals who find positive thinking and affirmations attractive are frequently people who have never felt powerful enough. At this level of development, they are exploring a sense of power. It is important to move into the stage where you begin to consciously direct the One Power. It is essential to growth if one is to understand power and its limits. Unfortunately, it has been bypassed by some groups in favor of letting go and letting God.

• *Should we stop imagining?*

It is not necessary to stop imagining. We work in concert with the One Power. There is a time to let go and a time to act. Everything we do, every thought we think, wields the power. Not to realize this fact is a result of spiritual ignorance. How is one to learn and grow unless one experiments and explores? Once you experience the miraculous powers of your mind and release the idea that you are separate from everyone and everything, you can then leave your imagination alone to do the work it does best, free to create in the present rather than in the future.

CONSCIOUS CHOICES

In my book, *The Lover in You, The Art of Imagining,* I dealt with the issue of how to make conscious choices in life. Making choices is an appropriate and important step for people who are past- or future-oriented. They need to have a starting point. Choice becomes very important for people who are afraid. They need to know they can make new choices that will improve the quality of their lives, especially if they feel the choices they made in the past were wrong. The experience of making a conscious choice and acting on it is a means of seeing things for what they are in order to be free of them. This opens the door for the real to be revealed.

- *How do we choose which beliefs or images to keep and which to discard?*

Why choose at all? Have you ever investigated why we choose? We only choose when we're confused. If we aren't clear about something, then we need to make a choice. Do you need to choose when you see something clearly? We make such a big deal of making choices. I'm not talking about choosing which clothes you're going to wear or what flavor of ice cream you're going to eat. I'm speaking about the kind of choices that come from mistrust and uncertainty. A mind that has no clarity must always choose. A clear mind has no choice and responds appropriately.

The real choice is not whether you **can** do something, but whether you **should** do something.

FREEDOM FROM BELIEF

The small assembly seemed receptive, and I felt very relaxed as I walked on stage. Scanning the audience, I noticed her. Self-confident and attractive, she was the only person dressed completely in black. As I spoke, she nodded her head in agreement, a wide smile on her face. At the end of my speech, she was the first to come up and tell me how much she had enjoyed the evening. She told me she agreed with everything I had said, and that she, too, believed in nothing. Appropriately, she was from Missouri, the "Show-Me" State. During the casual conversation, to demonstrate her lack of belief systems, she told me she didn't even believe the sun would rise the next morning until she saw it herself. "After all," she said, "it might not rise for me." I laughed and told her that wasn't freedom from beliefs, it was simply pessimism. In an instant, the smile was gone and I realized that she felt exposed. As she defended her position, I said nothing. She prided herself on being free from beliefs according to her *idea* of what that meant, and this belief formed what she felt was the very core of her identity. When the false identity was exposed, she became defensive. If she could have observed her reaction at that moment, she would have seen a truth about herself. Instead, by holding fervently to her position, she missed an opportunity to experience freedom in a way she had never experienced before.

We believe so many things on hearsay—in the faraway, in heavens and hells, gods and goddesses—because we've been told to believe in these things. We believe what we're told about ourselves, never bothering to verify this information. Freedom means letting go. Believing means holding on. Because beliefs give you the illusion of freedom, your most fundamental beliefs need to be questioned if you are ever to experience the letting go that real freedom brings. Once experienced, even briefly, you will be better able to distinguish between real freedom and the illusion of freedom.

The most limiting of all beliefs is that we are our body. From the belief in the body comes our perception of the world, and along with that, our perception of God, who is supposed to have created the world. Then fear begins, creating all kinds of systems to support and protect frightened children who, hiding in their little belief-system closets, are scared out of their wits by monsters of their own making. So they pray and begin to worship, which begets organized religion, which in turn demands sacrifice in one form or another.

One beautiful spring day, several friends invited me to attend Mass with them "just for the fun of it." When the time for communion came, I decided to take part. My friends were horrified. "You can't, you're not even Catholic," they said. They seemed to think the hand of God was going to strike me down. I wasn't taking communion to offend them. Since I was there, I wanted to participate fully in the service. It's not necessary to believe in a particular doctrine to enjoy the rituals. I thoroughly enjoyed taking part in the rites while they were too disturbed by my actions to take pleasure in the service.

There is a vast difference between being spiritual and being religious. Spirituality does not require a belief in a God or a system. It is the sense of the wholeness of things, a trust in life. Religion is a set of teachings, rules and conducts founded around a divine teacher, although religion can enhance spirituality if it is used constructively.

A friend of mine who is gay used to have a problem reconciling his sexual orientation with his religion. When he went to confession and told the priest what the problem was, the priest said, "The only sin is to deny what you are, what God made you." This young man was fortunate enough to have a very wise and understanding priest who helped him to accept himself. If he had gone to a priest who believed otherwise, those beliefs would have been imposed on him and he most likely would have continued to feel guilt and remorse for who he was. Any teaching that causes you to feel ashamed of yourself, your body, or your feelings is aggressive and abusive. It is insulting to your very being. You cannot be a whole person if you are constantly burdened with judgments about your actions or with bombastic commandments demanding adherence at the price of your integrity. You can "get" religion—many do and become religious gluttons—but you cannot "get" spirituality. You cannot follow its rules because it has none.

All religions and "special" groups hold out the promise of giving the individual a sense of being connected to something, of being a part of something greater than himself. The need to belong is a great motivator. Once a person is aware of being part of everything, it is unnecessary to go anywhere to feel a sense of belonging because you are already a part of wherever you may happen to be.

- ### *Aren't some New Age beliefs pathways to higher consciousness?*

The last couple of decades have seen a profound change in attitudes toward expanded states of consciousness, enlightenment and spirituality. The failure of our society to provide a fertile ground for the cultivation of one's self—its emphasis on materialism as opposed to community, of isolation rather than integration, of man as inherently "evil" rather than as intrinsically whole—has led to a mass turning toward Eastern and Native systems of philosophy and tradition as a means of salvation.

In typically Western fashion, the fascination with personal transformation has become virtually a national obsession, with gurus and recipes for enlightenment being hawked like cotton candy at a carnival.

In our enthusiasm we overlook the fundamental aspects of the teachings we embrace, with its seeming Catch-22 that requires us to be aware in order to be free. Without a firm sense of self, the unawakened consciousness senses the separation between the technique and the practitioner; it's unable to see that the effectiveness of any technique resides in one's self.

A self which is not conscious cannot be known. Consciousness creates itself from the position of its own existence; as it does, it moves slowly up to the stages of awareness. The way we view ourselves goes through developmental stages. Without complete movement through these stages, blending and balancing the parts into a whole, we're left with a sense of emptiness.

New Age and other current spiritual teachings, groups, courses, etc., offer one-sided formulas or recipes for living. The student replaces one set of beliefs for another, rather than inquiring into the nature of being. They give people beliefs to replace beliefs, doctrines to replace doctrines. It may be argued that there are "higher beliefs." While there may be some truth to this, the wise know that these beliefs, too, must be released. The bottom line is, beliefs are beliefs, period, and they keep people in a perpetual dream state.

You want your beliefs, what you refer to as your truth, confirmed by what your ordinary consciousness perceives as new and exciting sources. But it's important to see that all that you are capable of hearing at that ordinary level is that which you have already heard, that which reinforces the beliefs of your conventional consciousness. The "exotic" is not telling you anything new.

Psychologist Francis Vaughan points out, "the failure of orthodox religious practices to provide genuine experiences of transcendence have created a climate of spiritual deprivation and an intensified search for transcendental answers."

If there were such a thing as a "wrong" choice, the down side of it would be the psychological consequences of joining a group purportedly offering "spiritual" self-realization. According to a prominent transpersonal psychologist, large numbers of people are being led "to surrender self-determination willingly in order to gain a sense of purpose in a world perceived to be meaningless." We see individual quests for personal growth and spiritual fulfillment detouring through the shadow world of human potential, the noble desire for self-realization turned into a simple obsession with self-indulgence and immediate physical sensation; such excesses have led to a nationwide concern over cultism. Dr. Lowell Strieker addresses these issues by saying, "The cult controversy illumines not only conflicts of generation and values but shifts in perception about the way the world is, the way it will be, and what ought to be done about both."

People are hungry for any experience of what they think to be God, Kundalini or UFOs and are eager to believe just about everything they read or hear, if it fits in with what they want to be true. If the simple beliefs you have about yourself may be false, what makes you think these more encompassing beliefs might be true?

Kurt is a gifted sculptor whose artwork is admired by many, but he has difficulty making a comfortable, steady living. His personal earthly efforts are diffused by his otherworldly interests. His vivid imagination is a wonderful asset to his work, but it doesn't help him much in everyday life. He believes in flying saucers and claims it is the sign of an enlightened mind not to rule out the possibility of extraterrestrials. But for him, flying saucers are reality, not merely the acknowledgement of possibility.

So much in his life is unfulfilling that the fantastic and far-away holds greater appeal than his reality. He can't say that he has actually met an alien or been beamed aboard a spacecraft, but he likes the idea and wants it to be true. It helps to make him special. If he were content with his life, he might see things differently, but he's not content. He is always getting involved with one scheme or another requiring a hefty cash outlay, promising big returns that never materialize. Because he always looks on the bright side, he justifies these adventures as lessons. But he never does learn from them and continues to be sucked into one get-rich-quick scheme after another. In many ways, he is a very aware person, more so than many, yet he never seems to slow down long enough to see what he is doing.

In reading this example, you might think I am against these possibilities. I am not against them. I neither believe nor disbelieve them, which frees me for all possibilities without binding my energy to the belief process.

Many metaphysical people love words like "sacred places," "brotherhoods," the "light," and are conned by endless promises made in this workshop or group that they will meet their greater self, communicate with or see UFOs. This is all advertising. They promise that you will find out who you are, for a price. The price is not the money, but the energy wasted in useless pursuits. You want your old religions wrapped up in a New Age package but everything remains the same. You're still pursuing the same things, merely changing the façade. Now it's extraterrestrials, light brotherhoods, sacred places and conspiracies. I find it humorous when I look at our world and see the difficulty people have in tolerating anything that is new or anyone who is different, and yet there are so many who are eager to meet beings who might be *very* different indeed. Not only are most people unable to sustain a relationship with a member of the opposite or even same sex, they can barely tolerate their neighbor who happens to be of a different sexual, political, religious, ethnic or economic background.

It's important to see the commonness of it all. It's important to see how common *you* are—just one of the herd. And when you do find out that you've been taken for a ride, you justify it by saying you have learned from the experience. But you haven't. You were taken in by the same old thing—empty promises. And it's even more important to see that you will do it again. You're in love with anything that keeps you away from what is happening now, anything that prevents you from being who you are right now.

The power is not in the cards, the crystals, or in anything or anyone outside yourself. All power resides in the I AM of yourself. Within the I AM is the substantial, fundamental truth. Now I wouldn't necessarily take away someone's comfort but I am compelled to tell you that as long as you view the world through your belief systems, the outside is all illusion. It is not the reality that you take it for; it is a shadow of the reality—temporary, a pale copy. Only the essence is real. Start working with that as a basis and you will build upon a stable foundation. Understand, we are not here to change the world but to change our perception of the world; out of this comes our reality.

* *So you're saying that these beliefs are false?*

No. It's not for me to be your authority on the truth of what you may believe or disbelieve. You must be your own authority. Your beliefs may be true, or only partially so. I'm saying that if you want to be more conscious, aware and awakened (something which every one of you reading this book apparently wants or you wouldn't have read this far), then you must examine all you have ever taken to be true in order to find out for yourself what is true and what is not.

You think your beliefs serve you, but in what way? Have you investigated? Beliefs don't serve you; you serve them and you pay dearly for it. They are an investment in blindness. Believing yourself to be what you are not keeps you from being all that you are. Remember the woman from Missouri and her belief in her unbelief? Beliefs require an enormous amount of energy to sustain them, energy that you need if you want to go farther. It's a heavy price to pay. If you wish to become more aware, you can't afford it. That energy must be released. At a certain point, a person who wants to be more aware cannot continue to carry the burden of false beliefs. In order to climb to the top of the mountain where truth resides, he must first unload all the unnecessary baggage.

- *I feel I would fight and even die for what I believe in!*

Fight? Obviously. Die? I doubt it. Not intentionally, anyway. Willingness to die for something doesn't make it truer. What *is* true is that you're afraid to even consider the possibility that your beliefs may not be true and that's the truth you need to see. I admire your earnestness but your statement is foolish. If you must die, die for what is real. The fact that you refer to it as *your* truth suggests it is not *the* Truth. Your statement can't be verified, which makes it safe for you to say. It's like someone saying that they love humanity while not being able to be in a relationship with one other person. It's so easy to love the distant and the obscure. Love one other person and you will love many. Love yourself and you love everyone. I know you feel you'd die for what you believe in, but the next time you're placed in front of a firing squad for your beliefs, let us know what happens. It will hold more weight then.

The more emotional or sentimental you are, the less likely you are to examine your beliefs. This is detrimental to many New Agers and churchgoers. The example of a member of a group meeting at my house demonstrates this.

It had rained all day, and the moisture brought with it an uncomfortable chill. It wasn't a gentle rain, but a heavy downpour, the kind Southern California doesn't handle well. The group members were soaked by the time they entered the house, contributing to the uncharacteristically sober discussion at hand.

Pamela's expression betrayed the disturbance she felt as she sat cross-legged in a far corner of the room. She wanted to be perfect. She worked hard at it and didn't hesitate to correct you when your ideas and beliefs didn't coincide with her own. She belonged to a well-known group with a nasty reputation for aggressive persuasion and intimidation, yet for her it was the most superior of teachings.

"I'm twenty-three and I am a very spiritually advanced person. I am involved in a very spiritual organization and it bothers me that most of the people sharing here are coming from their heads. They're not coming from their hearts. Feelings are what is important if you want to be spiritual. I always come from my heart because that is the only way we can get in touch with our inner self. We should be sharing what we are feeling, not what we're thinking." Her attempt at piousness couldn't disguise her patronizing tone.

"Can you share from *your* feelings and let the others share intellectually, or must everyone come from the space you come from?" I asked. "You consider yourself to be spiritually advanced and yet admonish anyone who doesn't conform to your standard of behavior." This aggression within us, even if it is believed to be spiritually motivated, is why the world is as it is. Sentimental and emotional feelings (which we often refer to as coming from our hearts) are required to project what we believe *in*. The mind produces these feelings (energy) in order to anchor the illusion.

THE FUTILITY OF KNOWLEDGE

Unless you know from your own experience, all knowledge is futile. Knowledge has its uses, but it has been my experience that if I am going inward, it becomes more and more useless; the deeper I go, the more useless it is. The farther I go outward, the more useful it is. Knowledge is all the past. The future is conjecture. *Now* can only be experienced. I find that what we generally think of as knowledge is really information. Knowledge is borrowed, wisdom is my own, and only wisdom can transform you. People love to brag about their knowledge, but if our intelligence cannot show us the false phenomenon of the ego, then we're not very intelligent at all.

Wisdom comes when knowledge has been put aside. Call it knowledge or call it mind. Mind is knowledge. When you have put aside all knowledge, you are in a state of not-knowing. The state of not-knowing is difficult at first because we are so used to thinking we *know*. But it eventually becomes a beautiful experience because it is innocence. You will be full of wonder and awe. Giving up is the first step. But the real giving up is in realizing that there is nothing to give up. There's nothing to give up because nothing was ever ours in the first place.

4

MY QUEST
FOR FREEDOM

*"To know the truth, you must
pass through your own
experience in full awareness."*

As human beings, we have an innate desire for freedom. We want to be free from burdens, worries, lack, and the unsettling feeling of insecurity. Although we cling to the transient, we are conscious of the limited, tenuous and illusory character of our physical existence. We may envision the pleasures of this world to be real and satisfying, but pain and despair continually remind us otherwise. We try to believe that we will enjoy complete satisfaction once we've attained worldly things, but inwardly there is an unrelenting rebellion against this false belief. We intuitively know that we can only find satisfaction and complete peace by living in the present. Fueled by our desire for freedom, we have accomplished much in making the world a better place to live; however, there have always been limits to our freedom.

The cause of internal and external conflict in our lives is our assumption of and/or our quest for permanence. We would like to hold on to something predictable. Our mind would like to modify the world for reasons of convenience. When it can't make the external conditions more predictable and encounters the difference between what is and what the mind believes should be, we experience pain.

We search for freedom with a mind fragmented by beliefs which produces a world of duality where no peace, freedom or satisfaction can be found because only conflict arises from duality.

As long as we feel we are separate from each other, freedom will appear to be the ability to control and manipulate others. It doesn't take much of an expanded awareness to see that we usually associate freedom with money and/or success, which seems to lead to power, prestige and respect in the eyes of the world. But true internal freedom comes with the truth of what *is*. Only when we either willingly look at or are forced to face what *is,* are we liberated from these beliefs.

MY EXPERIENCE

I'd like to share my experience of how I came upon the potential of being free from beliefs, so I'll give a little history about how it all started.

I was born a lucid dreamer. A lucid dreamer is someone who is able to enter into dream states, particularly at night, and become conscious or awake in those dreams. These are not the dreams of the common mind, although sometimes that world is entered into or briefly touched by someone during sleep and will be remembered by them as being a very vivid dream. I didn't realize it was anything special until years later; I just enjoyed my dreams every night.

I was also an avid reader. As I grew older, I soon discovered books on magic and the occult. For years I read anything on metaphysics that I could get my hands on. Even when I worked as a dancer/actor on Broadway in New York City, I always carried a book to read during intermission. I knew there was something important in those books, if I could only grasp it, that would give me the answers to all life's questions, such as who am I? What's life all about?—

the usual questions.

When I moved to California, I stepped up my pursuit of the answers to these burning questions with even greater zeal. I became involved with many different groups and religions, but because I've always had the ability to really listen to what is being said and not get caught up in the personality of the individual conveying these messages, I was able to extract the gold and leave the rest. I saw other people getting caught up in the personalities rather than the message. I didn't have that problem—I didn't care who I listened to or what their personality or lifestyle was as long as I was learning something from them.

I became involved with a little-known organization that presented ideas—different beliefs, myths and ideas, religious and otherwise—to me, but they also gave me alternatives. They never told me what to believe in. They were very big on facts. They would say, "Now we don't know what this is, but the facts are ..." and they would present those facts. When it was a theory, they would say, "Now this is just a theory," then explain what the theory was and where it came from. They would present an idea or concept with all the information available on the subject, then stimulate the desire to experience it personally, rather than merely accepting it without investigation. After I left the group, I realized that what they were doing was training me to be open to seeing the oneness of life.

Eventually, however, I got to a point where I felt I knew too much. It was like an anchor around my neck, weighing me down. I was full of knowledge on a mental level, but unable to translate it to my life. I looked around and saw the same thing with the others involved in groups—as far as I could see, no one was really living what they were teaching. And I wondered what good all that knowledge was if it didn't lead to wisdom. I decided to just live my regular everyday life as best I could, so I proceeded to set aside all the books and information I had accumulated and to live the principles I'd learned.

These principles included the idea of responsibility, creative visualization, and positive thinking, as well as the more esoteric concepts of Zen and Buddhism. I wanted to experience these principles personally rather than merely read or talk about them. I felt a great urge to communicate these ideas to others, and I didn't want them discounting the ideas because I wasn't personally living them myself. I had already heard in other groups I was in: "Well, no, I can't really do it myself, but I can teach it to you." I wanted to live it myself so I could share from personal experience.

So, after discarding all the books, I spent about four or five years putting these beliefs into practice. I didn't particularly care if anyone else lived these principles or not. I wanted to do it—I wanted to live it, to experience it. If belief truly did create and produce in life, then I wanted to take my beliefs and prove it to my own satisfaction.

During this period, a dear friend named Alzada, an eighty-year-old woman, taught me a great deal. I remember asking her a question once that I thought very profound, very deep—something about the oneness of the Universe. And she just turned to me and said, "Is your rent paid?" I didn't know what she was talking about, so I asked the question again. Again, she turned to me and said, "Is your rent paid?"

I later realized the point behind her question: if your immediate, present world is not in order, there is no sense pursuing otherworldly interests. But we're in love with other dimensions of reality; we don't want to have to deal with what's here and now.

I had been told by a teacher whose name was Neville that "what is profoundly spiritual is also very practical," so I decided to put my beliefs into practical application, so that when I imagined something in my mind, it would produce itself in the world. I put images up on a bulletin board of all the things I wanted. I told myself if I truly believed these things about myself, my life, and the world and held true to those beliefs, keeping them constantly in mind, then I would produce them in my life. I was reconditioning myself to thinking positively, to thinking I can have anything I can visualize: a new car, a new life, a wonderful relationship, anything I want if I only believe it. And I did—I produced all of it.

I even started visualizing certain statements I wanted other people to say about me. For example, I was working out a lot, going to a gym and building myself up physically. Having always been thin and very self-conscious about it, I wanted to hear someone say, "God, you look great! You've really built yourself up." The next day, a total stranger walked up to me, hesitated, then turned to me and said, word for word, what I wanted to hear. When I realized how much my thoughts influenced the world, it frightened me for a while, but I continued visualizing over and over again.

I learned so much from doing this. I realized that every time we believe anything, we produce it in the world. Now it's not necessarily produced exactly the way we imagine, the basic belief is produced relative to the motive behind it. We bring our experiences into our life by believing them into existence.

Let me give you an example. People in life will often say they are waiting for another Jesus Christ, Buddha, or other master teacher to come into the world. But what they really want is a savior—someone to do for them what they cannot or will not do for themselves. They want to believe that someone is going to come and save them from all their sins, the horrors of the world, or whatever else they think they're bound by. That's a very natural thing for people to do, and when people want a savior, that's what they're going to get. For example, Hitler was a savior to the German people in the 1930s because they believed they needed someone to save them. They believed it and they produced it. Their savior came—they got Hitler. This may seem like an extreme example, but it can and does happen. It takes millions of people to believe a man like this into existence. We believe in something and we produce it, but by acting on the basis of our beliefs, which are backed by questionable motives, we live illusions which then create unfortunate consequences.

Another example: There came a point where I wanted to experience psychic phenomena—to travel to other worlds and have out-of-body experiences and all sorts of things like that—so I did. For several years I had incredible mystical experiences that were a definite step in my growth process. The more mystical experiences I had, the more I believed in them. And the more I believed in them, the more my mind produced them.

Then I started to grow again, and I moved from there into giving seminars on imagination and teaching people how to train their minds so that they would think constructively and produce a different life for themselves.

This may seem to contradict what I've been saying about beliefs, so let me explain further. In one sense, it is true that, when identified through feelings, our beliefs can be manifested. But one of the problems with having beliefs and one of the benefits of being free of them is that beliefs have boundaries. The very nature of a boundary means that there is something beyond it. If we only cling to the boundary, then we'll never go farther. Plato tells a story about people dwelling in a cave who only saw the outside world as the shadows cast upon the walls of the cave. One day a man left the cave, went outside and experienced the real world. Upon his return, the others didn't believe his report of things outside their knowledge and experience. But he was free from their belief that the cave was the only real world because he had experienced a wider reality and knew differently.

The way you view the world is not unlike being in a room of a large house that is situated on a hilltop. Let's say you are seated in the living room and there are four windows in that room. One window looks onto a small courtyard, one looks out at a neighbor's house, one faces north to a mountain range, and the main picture window has a view of the sky and the city below. Four people are looking through four different windows. They are in the same room, viewing the same world—in different ways. When asked to describe reality, the person looking at the courtyard might say, "The world is made up of flowers and a fountain and sunshine. It is rather small but very beautiful." The person looking out of another window will describe the world differently: "Oh, no. There is the wall of another house. There's a big tree shading the house and not much sunlight in this world. It's also unkempt, for the grass is overgrown and there are trash cans full of garbage sitting around. It's not a very pretty sight." Another sees a mountain range to the north. "There is a lot of potential in my world. I see mountain tops that I could climb." The fourth might say, "My world is really big. There's lots to see—a vast sky, an ocean, a big city with lots of people. There's a lot of diversity in my world."

While one view may be more expansive than another, all are valid and have some truth but none of them is the complete truth. You may encourage a person to look through a different window, but he is still in only one room of the house. I could tell you about other rooms in the house, and you may or may not believe me. The young girl who says she is very spiritual may be looking out of a bigger window; this may give her the feeling of spiritual superiority, but she's still confined to the living room.

Our teachings and organizations are like many rooms and windows in the same house. Each room is different, and each has windows with various views, but they are still *in* the house. When you recondition or reprogram yourself, you are exchanging the view from one window for another, or even moving to a different room, but you are still in the house. You have changed your belief and expanded yourself, but you are still limited. You will always be limited within the confines of the house. I am encouraging you to leave the house altogether and move outside; to be under the sky, not a roof; to be out in the fresh air, not in a stale room. Beliefs are the walls surrounding a confined space. No matter how big the room, all belief has a boundary, which makes it limited. Have no walls. Neither believe nor disbelieve. Be open and available. Be alive.

Here's another example to help you further understand states of consciousness. Let's imagine a map of the United States. You are on the East Coast and you want to reach the West Coast because you've heard about the Pacific Ocean and you want to experience it. The Pacific Ocean represents the vastness of freedom and full awareness. So you begin your journey, one state at a time. Each state is a little different from the previous one because the people of each state think differently and the laws of each state are different as well. A law that might apply in New York may not apply in Ohio. What is true in Ohio is not necessarily true in Colorado, but they are similar because they are all part of a greater country called America.

So, off you go. Obviously, in order to enter a state, you must be willing to leave the previous state. Sometimes it is difficult because each state (idea, belief, religion) has a certain allure. But your inner longing is to reach the West Coast, no matter how sidetracked you may become at times. While traveling through the different states, you take with you all the accumulated knowledge you have gained. These souvenirs take up room and weigh your luggage down; it becomes heavier and heavier. After some time, you reach Nevada and enter Las Vegas with all its glittering lights and delights. This is the psychic world—the world of channeling, fortune tellers, astrologers, and extraterrestrials. It's unlike any other state you've visited.

You feel this must be what you've really been looking for. You feel power like you've never felt before. It's fun and exciting. You think you've arrived. That's the biggest danger to those who are journeying to the West Coast. The allure of Vegas is the most difficult to move beyond. It all seems so real. Most people stay in this state a very long time. A few eventually see the illusion, and realize that although the experience is valid while you are in Las Vegas, it is not the reality you originally sought. So, with much effort and determination, you leave Nevada and continue to the Coast. It is not gaining these powers that is the benefit of the experience—it is the ability to release that power after you have attained it.

Finally, you get a glimpse of the mighty Pacific. How do you explain that glimpse to people who are landlocked? How do you explain vastness and freedom to people surrounded by the boundaries of walls? You finally reach the shore and the ocean is before you. It's unlike anything you could imagine, so different from the stories you'd heard. But how do you travel in it? You can't take a car or a bus or a train. None of those apply here. No belief system applies. There are no landmarks, no paths—just vastness. This is water, not land. How do you leave the country itself behind?

This story illustrates the journey we as individuals must take. So you set out, going through many states of consciousness on the way. Now I define a state of consciousness as everything we believe, accept, and most importantly, consent to as being true. Because it seems to be true, we think it ceases to be a belief. For us, it becomes a fact, even though it's a belief and not a fact.

Now, the fact may be true, it may be partially true or it may be a complete superstition or fantasy. The human mind is filled with so many of these beliefs, it's a wonder anyone could move past the boundaries. Yet it is possible. There are those who have done it. I've done it to a certain degree, which is why I encourage people to move beyond the boundaries and free themselves from beliefs. I don't mean just the little beliefs about moving from lack to prosperity, from hate to love, from one belief to another. I'm talking about not reprogramming yourself. This is the basis of this book: not reprogramming or reconditioning yourself. Can a person neither believe nor disbelieve and, letting go of where he is, not add a different belief? Is it possible? I say it is.

Most people are afraid to let go of their beliefs because, for a while, they feel as if they are not rooted to anything. But that's what freedom is. People say they want freedom, but what they really want is just a little freedom. The boundaries of their beliefs may be pretty large, and they may seem to be free, but sooner or later, they'll run up against the limits of their belief. Why not sooner rather than later? Why not today—why not now?

I started this book by saying, "I believe in everything and

I believe in nothing." Now that really confuses people. They say, "Now wait a minute, you're being contradictory." What they don't understand is, it's not contradictory. If their eyes were open and aware, they would begin to see the world is both one vast contradiction and no contradiction at the same time. Believing in nothing frees you to believe in everything. In a sense, they cancel each other out.

So, going back to my story, I taught these seminars for a while, then I began writing for several metaphysical magazines. This was during the time New Age ideas became popular throughout the country and not just at esoteric gatherings. I became reasonably well-known and received invitations to speak at seminars, conferences and the large metaphysical Expos, as well as on television. I considered myself fortunate that I was able to speak to so many different groups of people because, in their own special way, they all related to what I was sharing. They always thought of me as being a member of their own particular organization, whether it be Catholic, Science of Mind, Alcoholics Anonymous, or esoteric metaphysics.

While I was writing for a certain magazine, I became friends with the editor, a man from India. One night, he called me to question a statement I had made in my article.

"You don't really believe that, do you?" he asked.

"Believe what?" I said.

"That statement—you don't *really* believe that?" He sounded so incredulous that I found myself reacting.

I said, "Well, I don't believe it. It's a fact."

He began to laugh, and said, "What makes you think this

is a fact?"

We debated for over three hours. It had been so long since anyone had questioned what I said that it pushed a button in me. I remember getting angry and upset because he didn't accept what I was saying as the truth. As we were arguing, I realized he was telling me this was a belief.

As I hung up the phone, my life changed immediately. It was a transcendent experience, an illumination, and I discovered that transformation is something that takes place in an instant. It's not something occurring over a period of time. The actual transformation happens instantly. It was like I became illuminated as soon as I hung up that phone. I sat there and I thought, "Oh my God, if that's a belief and I took it as a fact, what about everything else I think factual? How many of them are really beliefs?" I became confused and sat up the whole night wondering whether the things I had been teaching as fact were, in actuality, beliefs.

I had made a quantum leap from one level to an entirely different level, questioning literally everything I had ever thought I knew. I began to feel that I knew nothing. It was as though my whole life had been spent as a safely anchored ship, and now I was set adrift. I went through that period for several weeks.

One morning, I woke up and realized that there are so many different levels that what's true on one level is not necessarily true on another level. (Ultimately, there are no levels. Everything is "one," but for the purpose of explanation, the concept of levels is sometimes used.) I felt completely refreshed and free of everything. I walked outside and was overwhelmed by the simplicity of life. It dawned on me that there is no purpose to life other than what we give it. I looked at a flower and saw the interconnectedness, the oneness of life. I thought, there's no purpose, no reason for anything and it just is what it is. Life doesn't need a reason to exist.

The feeling of freedom that came over me was like nothing I had ever experienced. My mind was free—it didn't have to come up with explanations or ideas or beliefs. I felt so fresh and so new. There was no need to look to anything or look forward to anything. It was as though I had seen life for the first time. I felt connected to every aspect of life, but without the sense of urgency or need for accomplishment I had always known. My mind wasn't there. It was a sense, it wasn't a thinking process. It was a sense, a feeling, a fragrance of life. It was what psychologists describe as a "felt" experience, something that can't really be explained verbally. How do you explain the fragrance of a rose to someone who has never smelled one? What words do you use?

I felt myself becoming progressively lighter. Waves of raw emotion rose and fell within me, liquid feelings flowing through my being that filled me up and carried my heart away. I felt as though I were safely resting in gentle hands. I knew at once that I was safe, that we are all safe and always have been. It's an astonishing realization that has nothing to do with wanting or needing to be secure. You just know that you are secure; there is no question about it.

The experience left me a humbler and wiser man. I found it difficult to share because there were no words to describe what I had seen and felt, yet I was changed in many ways.

I began to allow this sense of deepening freedom within my being to penetrate me profoundly. I became willing to let myself be shaken in my familiar and secure beliefs, to allow myself to be troubled enough to renew my inquiry into myself and what I lived for.

I'd read about this process and understood it on an intellectual level, but had never experienced it. Indeed, I really wasn't aware that I had never experienced it—I'd always thought I was completely aware and in touch with reality. Until I was free, I didn't realize how unfree I had been. That's when I really began to examine where I was.

- *How can any of what you say be proven?*

If I could give you the proof you want—which I can't—your belief would be based on my proof, not your own. You would end up back where you started. My experience is my proof and is valid only for me. I can only share that experience with you as best I can through the limited medium of words. You can't have my experience—who can have another's experience? Instead of spending valuable energy looking for proof of the truth, which you do not know, see the reason why you need external proof.

- *But how can I know that what you say is true?*

You're still looking for outside proof. To know the truth, you must pass through your own experience in full awareness. You can know what is *not*. What *is,* you can only be. Investigate the proofs you have of what you believe you know. You'll find you know nothing for sure. You just believe what you've been told.

5

THE BENEFITS OF FREEDOM

*"We are such strange beings.
We don't understand the
common things of life,
the simple struggles and joys,
and yet we try to grasp
the mysterious and hidden."*

The transformation that occurs when an individual makes a quantum leap to a higher energy level produces a radical shift in understanding that may be followed by major changes in the individual, such as increased awareness, leading to physical and psychological healing. This new level of energy and awareness generates new relationships with all aspects of our lives. The transformation I am talking about begins with scrutinizing our life, our beliefs, ourselves.

Physicists tell us: "You cannot observe anything without changing the object and even yourself." Most of us are quite willing to scrutinize someone else's life and judge it by our highly self-esteemed opinion. But can we observe our own lives?

On more than one occasion, we have experienced how observation generates self-transformation and transcends habit patterns. When there is full awareness, we create room for spontaneity. It is in this space that insights occur to give us the freedom to drop our habits instantly. Unless habits cease, there is no possibility of change.

This ability to observe ourselves has been shared with us by many illumined men and women. What could be simpler than to look at something and see it for what it is? I have not yet found anyone—not even a Buddha, a Christ, or any kind of revered master—who was not required to undergo the fires of thought purification before developing the ability to *see*. To truly see, we must first clear our inner vision of the beliefs that cloud our perception of ourselves and our world.

Life is a monologue, a soliloquy played out through our relationships with ourselves, our world and with others; the world and the seeming other *is* us. When we realize this, we either become remorseful and (consequently) vindictive and skeptical, or we take responsibility for our world by way of the ideas we entertain—self-pity dissolves and in its wake we find confidence and self-esteem.

If we can remain alert long enough to see the faults, hypocrisy and the errors in our particular belief system— see it totally as it is and rise above it by not judging it—then our lives will no longer be guided by the forces of duality—such as attraction/repulsion, friendship/enmity, pleasure/pain—but by the simple urge to give ourselves to the moment, free from purely selfish desires.

RESISTANCE TO ACTION

Belief inhibits action. When you analyze and question an action, you put an end to it. When you're aware, your actions become very intense because you're giving it your total self. Your being moves appropriately with that action. It's almost as if there were no choice, which is a good thing because choice is only for people who have belief systems. You become free of having to make choices because you move appropriately with life. You never do anything that's inconsistent with the reality of who you are.

Because we can't see clearly all the time, we go other places or turn to other things or other people.

A woman I counseled wanted everyone to do everything for her. She felt incapable of any action on her own. I told her repeatedly that only she could make her own changes, no one else could do it for her. She thought if she could only find the right place, read the right book or meet the right person who would wave a magic wand over her, things could change and transformation would occur. She'd been to countless psychologists, doctors, groups, read numerous books, and was still looking for a secret key. I told her the only magic route to transformation lies through direct action, but my words fell on deaf ears—it wasn't what she wanted to hear.

Another man was addicted to Biblical and New Age quotes. He said he believed in the truth of these sayings and he could quote endless phrases, but he couldn't live them.

Why do people think this information holds more weight if it is channeled or comes from some hidden manuscript or lost scroll? It's so simple that the mind dismisses it. The mind cannot comprehend simplicity. It wants everything to be extremely complicated. Freedom from believing requires that you live in a totally unknown universe.

People need to see the obvious: only they can live their lives; no one else can live their lives for them. Until they can overcome their mental and spiritual laziness, they will remain stuck.

They are not alone. Lots of people, lacking a sense of self-direction and self-responsibility, want someone or something else to do for them what they need to do for themselves. Let Jesus or Buddha save me. Give me a miracle. Let the Universe do it.

THE ABILITY TO SEE

There are steps in the ordinary flow of consciousness that we instinctively feel compelled to take. Many of us feel a sense of loss when we realize that our beliefs no longer define us. Some of us give up, content to be discontent, dismally experiencing *what is* as what it's not.

Others, sensing that this is the train's last stop before pulling into Sunset Village, join the gym, change their hairstyles, even their lifestyles. They sell their big-city house and move to the country to commune with nature. They quit the corporate rat-race and stay home to write the great American novel. Their children almost grown or out of the nest, they trade in a familiar, sometimes uncomfortable relationship with their spouse for the allure of a mysterious stranger. Such external changes may boost flagging self-esteem and even fulfill some vital needs, but the ring they grasp is made of brass, not gold, as they discover upon closer examination.

Others still hear the internal voice whispering its profound longing. Dr. M. Scott Peck, in "The Road Less Traveled," says this voice utters "the call to grace. . . . a call out of spiritual childhood into adulthood."

Some people will start making what will appear to be conscious choices and act on those choices; others will become more choiceless as they begin to slow down and stop rushing through life. There are people who are ready to explore and release the beliefs that no longer serve them; others will need to have something to believe in. Some will move into a silent period while others will open up and share more.

There are those who will need to stop disciplining themselves, to stop trying to be so consistent and experience a period of permitting themselves to "happen." While some need to enter into their feelings more, others will have to begin having some control over their emotions, because at a certain point, human emotion has to be brought under a degree of control. And still others, must start to "think"—to learn to use their minds—not more intellectually, but more intelligently.

FREEDOM OF EXPRESSION

A child at play, full of laughter and tears, running and jumping, yelling and singing, is marvelous to watch. And watching her was about all I had the energy to do. A local television news station had proclaimed the day as "the hottest in years," as if I needed his verification. Resting in the shade, barely able to move, afforded me the opportunity to observe her silently as she played, expressing herself fearlessly moment to moment, completely uninhibited and seemingly unaffected by the hot, dry Santa Ana winds.

Expressing one's self can be frightening for most people. I remember an acting class I attended many years ago in New York City. The two actors on stage were doing one of the most boring scenes I had ever witnessed. It wasn't the fault of the material they were performing; it was them.

"What do you think you're doing up there?" the teacher asked them.

After a long pause, one of the actors shyly suggested, "Acting?"

We all laughed.

"We're trying to be real," added the other actor. "I don't want to over-act."

"What do you people think real is?" the teacher inquired. "Certainly not the behavior most people display in their everyday lives. Out there, everyone is repressed, and you think that is an example of real life? As actors, it is our responsibility to express ourselves in a way that everyday people do not because they are too self-conscious. You're not here to be self-conscious. A little over-acting would do you a world of good and hold your audience's attention a whole lot more. They don't pay to come to the theater or go to a movie to see what they can see in their everyday lives. They come to the theater to feel something. They come to see someone express themselves in a way they feel they cannot. Everyone wants to express himself but almost everyone is deathly afraid to do it."

There was momentary silence in the room, then the teacher said, "Now, start the scene again, and for God's sake, give it some life. Take some chances, show some passion, stop playing it safe. Express yourselves!"

One of the biggest freedoms we experience upon releasing belief is the freedom of expression. If you're free to express, you're free to discover all sorts of new things—about yourself, other people, the world around you. You exude it and it's catching. Other people like to be around you because they can sense that energy and it allows them to express themselves more completely.

For years, I produced hundreds of conscious images as I practiced the principles I had learned about how the One Power operates through the brain. I was really into imaging a better life for myself, both physically and psychologically. I worked hard, concentrating on what I wanted, thinking positively. After years of controlling my emotions and thoughts, I was tired of the constant discipline. I was sure there must be some way to encompass all the individual images and desires into one basic image. Finally, I realized that all my wants and desires could be summed up in a very simple and direct way. I wanted to be able to express myself.

This was a great revelation to me. I had been trying to discover what would make me happy—what people, places and things—and how that happiness would ultimately be attained. At that point, I entered into the state of expressing myself 100 percent in everything I did.

What it all comes down to is that people want to express themselves, whether through a relationship, wealth, success or spirituality. Music, painting, dance, poetry and prose are the soul's expression of the muse. Whether you find your expression in the creation of such art or in its enjoyment, you want the ability to express that self. If people are able to express themselves totally—in their feelings, in their talents, in their being—they are happy. Yet as long as they are bound by their belief systems, they are not able to express themselves fully because they have no idea who they really are.

FREEDOM TO LOVE

Shortly after I had gone through the experience of transcending beliefs, one of my oldest friends was in the hospital, desperately ill. He had been attending a well-known metaphysical group and was an avid student of the particular course they followed. I was with him when he experienced a crisis and the doctors and nurses were trying to help him. In his fear, he stubbornly refused their help. He yelled that the Universe would take care of him. I think he thought that help was just going to drop out of the sky or something. Frustrated and angry, I said, "Who do you think the Universe is? It's this doctor and this nurse and me—all of us who are trying to help you. We are the Universe."

His belief had separated him from reality, which was that the Universe he revered so much worked through people.

Anyway, I stayed with him all night long. About three o'clock in the morning, I suddenly had the sensation that he was surrounded by a group of beings. Very clearly, I heard a voice in my head saying, "It's a gathering of angels."

Those who know me know that I am very grounded and try to help other people be grounded. It's not that I do or do not believe in the possibility of angels, it's simply that I prefer to allow my experience to be genuine and not the product of a vivid imagination or a particular belief system. One of the wonderful things that results from being free of belief systems is that you simply experience the moment without getting caught up in it. So I was able simply to be there and have the experience without having to cart around a belief in angels or beings from another world. It happened, I accepted it. I was open.

I couldn't get the voice out of my head for weeks. It kept saying, over and over, "a gathering of angels." It never said what a gathering of angels was, but an idea was instilled in me. Shortly before my friend's illness, I had come to the realization that I didn't know what I believed and what I didn't, so I decided to start a group. I wanted to invite people who wished to experience greater personal and spiritual freedom in their lives, so I had started to design an announcement when I realized I didn't know what to call the group. Now, a few short weeks later, I had a name.

So I put the announcement in my newsletter. The idea was to gather a group of people who were on the path of growth and share our thoughts, ideas, feelings—in short, ourselves—and just be present in the moment. No leaders, no followers, just people exploring the path of enlightenment or just sharing our experiences and feelings with each other. I knew what I needed was not to teach but to find out what belief systems I had retained unknowingly.

Eight people attended the first meeting. Most, if not all, had attended a metaphysical event called the Harmonic Convergence, which was intended to bring about world peace. In other words, they considered themselves extremely spiritual and advanced. I introduced a subject and let the discussion start rolling on its own.

As people spoke, they used what I call metaphysical buzzwords: love, peace, harmony, consciousness, and so on. As they grew more comfortable in the setting, I saw these spiritual, peaceful beings grow more heated in their attempts to outdo each other with the quality of their metaphysical knowledge. It virtually became a free-for-all.

Finally, I could stand it no longer and said, "Look at the eight of us. We're supposed to be so spiritually advanced that we presume to teach others how to live more harmoniously, yet we cannot gather in one room and keep peace amongst ourselves. It's ridiculous." I was laughing because the situation reminded me of certain wildlife specials I had seen on television—not the ones about cute little bunnies, but the wild and woolly dangerous ones—and I thought, instead of calling the meeting "A Gathering of Angels," I should call it "A Gathering of Potentially Dangerous Animals." I had attempted to provide a safe place where people could discuss their ideas and concepts in peaceful non-aggression and instead I found these spiritual barracudas going for each other's throats.

In the course of that evening and the years of gatherings that followed, I learned an awful lot from this group about love, whether they were aware of it or not. It was part of the freedom I had gained. When you have those moments of freedom, you experience this thing called love, and with it comes compassion and understanding. You don't condone anything. You simply understand it. You protect yourself if necessary, but you understand. And this understanding only comes with freedom from belief systems.

Although I had no belief system to follow, no structure I was trying to teach, nor was I desirous of learning or inventing a new one, I continued having the group each week. It was an education in people's motivations, desires and beliefs. I saw, despite their self-proclaimed spirituality (or maybe because of it), the very strongest barriers against freedom from belief exist in people who consider themselves spiritual. They bandy a lot of words about but don't really understand their meaning.

The daughter of a well-known actress and metaphysical speaker and author, Colleen had come to the gathering one evening at the insistence of a friend. Settling into the sofa, she glanced around the room, defying those present to tell her something she didn't already know. After all, she was her mother's daughter, and had absorbed her mother's teachings, and that was more than enough. Besides, did we know *who* she was?

Throughout the evening she constantly talked about love—loving people, loving humanity, and how we just have to love, love, love. Her aggressiveness and insensitivity to those around her told me this woman knew nothing about love, but she used the word and believed she understood love. Intellectually, she did. She had been to lots of seminars and had read many books, so she was filled with knowledge and mistook that knowledge for understanding. When I asked, "Can you tell me what you mean by love," she stumblingly said, "Well, you know, Love." I could hear the capital letter as she reverently said the word, as if it explained something.

Many metaphysical people talk a great deal about love. It's easy to claim belief in something and think that means you are living it, but words are not substitutes for action. People talk a great deal about right action, but unless the mind is free of ideas and beliefs, it cannot act rightly. The highest form of sensitivity, love is vulnerable and receptive. It can only be lived. If you are talking a great deal *about* it, you probably aren't living it. This book is about love. You cannot love through your beliefs, because beliefs separate us. So, if you observe yourself talking a lot about love, it's probably time to start doing.

FREEDOM FROM EGO

We want our beliefs to be true because they define us, make us special. *Look how special I am. If you believe the way I do, you're okay, otherwise you're an outsider. Only my belief is the Truth.* It is this belief in the specialness our beliefs confer on us that brings us to the Ego.

A self-styled "spiritually advanced" man attended the gathering once. Eric arrived late, which enabled him to make a grand entrance. He didn't come to learn; he came because he felt he had "arrived" and was there to share his presence and knowledge with others. He had no interest in listening or observing the truth about himself. He only wished to monopolize the discussion with his ideas and opinions. We had been talking about the roles we play in life, and everyone shared but him. After a moment, I turned to him and asked, "Why the image of the holy man when it's hard enough just being anyone?" He said nothing, but his face turned bright red. It was evident that he suddenly saw himself clearly and realized he was fooling no one but himself.

The Ego has to be right. Believing has a great deal to do with being right. It reinforces our opinion of ourselves as being right, therefore being good or special or elite. When people become free of beliefs, they have reached the point where their Ego doesn't need the outside reinforcement and verification of another's definition of who they are. They have their own insights and become their own authorities about what they do, think and believe. They have what I call freedom from the need to win, which allows them to release deeply rooted ideas and free their egos from the need to be right. Because they no longer need to be right, they are free to share openly and allow others to share freely as well. Their ego no longer gets in the way. There's no longer any need for elitism.

I'm reclining in my swimming pool while working on this book. The sky is clear and it's a beautiful day. The temperature is about 80 degrees. The water feels great. I'm looking at the fruit on the tree in my backyard. What more could I desire? Why do I need to believe in anything? What need do I have to convince myself that I believe in life after death, or any other belief? I'm here. I'm alive and in the present—what could be more wonderful?

I don't have to believe in this swimming pool. Complex and sophisticated theories emerging in contemporary cognitive psychology view all of our waking experience of "reality" as only an approximation of the sensory world. Maybe, on some deep level, the swimming pool is an illusion and I believe in that illusion. But it doesn't matter. The pool is here and I don't have to keep saying, "I believe in a swimming pool and I believe I'm in the pool." It's not necessary. Awake and aware of every moment and everything that is happening, I'm content simply with being here and now.

This business of what is real and what is illusion can be confusing. Think of it this way: Stand in front of a mirror. You are real and so is the mirror, but your image reflected in the mirror *isn't* real. The ego is unreal but the thought process, brain cells and memories *are* real. It's when consciousness becomes identified with the brain cells (the mirror) that the ego (the reflection) is formed. The more aware you become, the less you are affected by this false ego that interferes with everything. It's no longer threatening to realize that you are powerless about certain things or that you have limitations. The false ego wants to think it has no limits, but it does. As your awareness grows, there will be no false ego to make judgments about the past. You will see the past clearly and be free of it.

FREEDOM TO BE REAL

> *"When you are Real you don't mind being hurt. ... It doesn't happen all at once," said the Skin Horse. "You become. It takes a long time. That's why it doesn't often happen to people who break easily, or have sharp edges, or who have to be carefully kept. Generally, by the time you are Real, most of your hair has been loved off, and your eyes drop out and you get loose in the joints and very shabby. But these things don't matter at all, because once you are Real you can't be ugly, except to people who don't understand."*

> *—"The Velveteen Rabbit"*

Like the Skin Horse told the Rabbit, becoming real "takes a long time." Just about the time most of our hair has vanished and we get "loose in the joints," we realize there is something still missing. Outwardly, we appear to be mature individuals, yet inside we feel a sense of incompleteness, a yearning for something as yet unknown. "Are we real yet?" we wonder.

Our time until now has been spent making our mark on the world. Now we become aware of a frozen void within us; we feel hollow and unfulfilled. There must be something more, we think. We once more question the meaning of our existence.

This is in part brought on by the realization that we are no longer young. We are not yet old, but the first blush of youth is no longer upon us: our physical reactions are not as quick as they once were and our thinking processes seem to take longer than before. We become more aware of our own mortality and begin to lose the youthful certainty that old age and death are part of someone else's life, not our own. We begin to see, as author Gail Sheehy puts it, "the dark at the end of the tunnel." Growing older is like watching the sun going down. As it nears the horizon, it seems to descend faster. The proximity to death seems closer as we age, so life seems to go faster.

Part of becoming free from beliefs includes coming to terms with our inner self. In doing so, we begin to be whole and wholly alive, moving from our limited consciousness of belief to an awakened consciousness. In the struggle to reconcile ourselves with ourselves, we must connect with the powerful forces of destructiveness and creativity coexisting in the human soul, and integrate them in new ways. This can only be accomplished when we are no longer blinded by belief.

In our search, we experience a crisis that leads to personal transformation of spiritual awakening, and ultimately to the wisdom of our inner-connectedness with the community of life. The purpose of this crisis is to educate the soul in becoming real.

The Chinese word for "crisis" is comprised of two symbols, one meaning "danger," the other "opportunity," a reminder that crisis has a positive as well as a negative aspect.

On higher levels of consciousness, AIDS might be considered a necessary experience, but to the people who are experiencing it and those who are close to them, it is very traumatic. I'm no stranger to the subject, having facilitated several HIV groups through the years. I've also been personally affected by it through loved ones who have died or are currently experiencing it.

Many metaphysical people, in an attempt to be helpful, say things like "You created this," or, "It's only an illusion." Others impose their own beliefs (especially about wrath and punishment) that only confuse or anger a person experiencing a life-threatening illness. When someone is in pain or discomfort physically, emotionally or mentally, that pain demands all their attention. Words don't help. Frequently, the words of solace we speak are more to comfort ourselves than the one who is suffering, because their pain reminds us of our own mortality. Those who say "Illness is an illusion" will find that statement isn't much help when they are actually living with constant pain. It's easy to say "I'm not afraid of death" when it is another's experience you are talking about. Such bold statements go right out the window during any real experience of one's mortality.

Steven was in his mid-twenties but looked much older. He had just completed college and was out on his own for the first time. He was open and receptive, devoid of any pretense. He was real. He had AIDS.

"Do you feel you did anything wrong to bring this about, such as making the wrong choices?" I asked.

"Perhaps, but I don't think so," he said thoughtfully.

"I hope that you are able to realize, at least in theory, that this probably was not a conscious choice in the way some people would have us believe," I told him.

"I just don't want to fight any more," he replied, sadness and spent anger in his voice.

It is the nature of some people to fight. They are born warriors, fighting for everything in life. When they get a life-threatening disease, they will fight to the end. It's the nature of others to be passive. When experiencing a crisis, they surrender to it more easily. One way is not right or more admirable than the other; it is simply the way that particular person handles life. My observation is that AIDS may be a disease having more to do with living than with dying. Dying is easy; living is difficult—we don't really know what will happen next. We like to think we do, but we don't. AIDS helps to reveal the personality that was always there. From the standpoint of higher consciousness, it may actually be a fortunate experience because it compels a person to see, appreciate and respond to life in a way they may not have experienced before. It makes a person real.

When a person experiences pain and discomfort from moment to moment without trying to escape it, something changes inside him. It's like a long-distance runner who, exhausted and in pain, reaches a point where endorphins are released. Even though his body is struggling, he moves into a place of peace. The pain is still there, but he becomes separated from it and continues to run. This is not really an escape; it's a higher state of being.

FREEDOM FROM FEAR

Your beliefs chain you to the past. The minute you say you believe something, it's already the past. You're basing your belief on something you heard or saw a minute ago, a year ago, ten years ago. It's always the past. You can only be free in the present. You can't be free in the past, you can't be free in the future. You can only be free right now. Right this moment. You can only be liberated right now.

I said earlier that our beliefs are based on fear. We believe because we're actually afraid. That's the bottom line. Fear is something that can only exist relative to something. Yet, many times when I ask what someone is afraid of, they'll say what they're really afraid of is the unknown. I tell them that's impossible. You can't be afraid of the unknown. You can only be afraid of what you know or of losing what you know. Fear is always in relation to the known, not the unknown.

This fear of what we know is based on our past experiences. For example, we remember a time when we were hurt or abandoned or something unpleasant happened. Then we're afraid of the future, because we're afraid that's going to happen again. Our continual projection of these ideas and beliefs into the future ensures that what we're expecting will come to pass.

The fear of losing what we know occurs when you lose the association you have with the familiar. An example of this is fear of death. People think they are afraid of death because it is unknown. I suggest that the real fear is of losing what you know.

One evening, after the gathering had dispersed, Gerri remained. She was emotionally vulnerable, longing for love but afraid to love because she was afraid to lose. She kept saying, "No one loves me." As I took her hand, I could feel her stiffen. I put my hand on her shoulder and she recoiled. I asked her, "How can anyone love you? Love is not permitted to enter into you—you've already said no. Love is all around you. If you're sensitive, you can feel it everywhere, but you can't feel it because you are so closed."

"How can anyone love me? I'm so fat; all I do is eat. I've never gotten over my father's death. Every man I meet eventually leaves. Even friends don't seem to stay long. So I get depressed, and when I'm depressed, I eat. The problem is that I *always* feel depressed, so I'm always eating."

"Obsession with food is a love need," I said as we walked outside. "If you are loved and can love in return, you will eat less. Love fills you up so much, you won't feel empty."

Lots of people have a "fear of abandonment" issue, which leads to problems in relationships. They're afraid to get close to other people, because they're afraid they are going to be abandoned. I told her perhaps she should get a nice cuddly dog or cat to keep her company. It would love her unconditionally and help ease her fears of abandonment. She loved animals, but she didn't want to get a pet because she said eventually the animal would die and leave her. She was afraid of that. She said there was no point in loving something for years, only to have it die.

Well, she's already dead. She's so afraid of being hurt that she can't enjoy something while it's here because, in her mind, she wants it to last forever.

This issue of things lasting forever surfaced the other day with a friend of mine. Bill was talking about how the turmoil in his life had vanished and now everything was smooth sailing. He thinks life will stay nice and calm, no more turmoil. I suggested that everything moves in cycles, from high to low and back again. "Life is like a wild river, Bill. It's wild sometimes, it's calm at times and then it goes into the rapids again."

He didn't like that; he thought that I was being negative. It's not negativity to look at life as it is, and to see that life is always changing. He wanted it to get to a certain point and stay there.

This desire for constancy is a major problem for many people. It is one of the reasons people hang onto their beliefs. They want to believe in permanence, in things always being good. If things aren't, then something must be wrong. But there's no freedom in that. How can you be free when your mind is so filled with all these conditions based on fear?

Fear dulls the heart. It also dulls the mind. When you're afraid, you don't really think about what's happening, you simply react. There's no intelligence involved. It's impossible to rise above fear through suppression or discipline or any kind of will power. It can only be transcended when you discover your beliefs, release them and understand the cause of your fear, then face the fear.

I'm not talking about rational physical fears, such as the fear of fire. It's not the fire you fear, which can bring warmth and comfort by heating our homes and cooking our food. Instead, we fear the power fire has to injure and destroy. These are rational fears. What I am talking about is psychological fear, which is always related to the past and the future, never the present.

When people transcend their beliefs, they move into a timeless state where they are very much in the present and at peace with themselves and the world around them. Once we accept that fear exists, we can then move beyond it and experience that indescribable stretching of being, the alchemy that transforms *chronos* (measurable time) to *kairos* (the timeless, infinite moment).

A FEW MORE BENEFITS

It requires courage to move beyond the boundaries of your beliefs, but there are many benefits. In addition to all the freedoms mentioned in this chapter, you'll also experience a sense of increased self-worth because you will begin trusting your own perceptions more; you will have less need for others to agree with you. You will have fewer feelings of anger, anxiety and depression because you will be disclosing your real self in more spontaneous ways. Your relationships with others will be better—more effective and more satisfying—because you will neither need to approve of their beliefs nor receive their approval. You will have achieved a profound philosophical change and a radically new outlook on life instead of a "positive thinking" attitude that will only help you cope temporarily with life.

All these benefits can be stated in one word: Freedom.

6

THE GATEWAY TO TRANSFORMATION

*"Live and love dangerously.
Even if you only manage
a single real moment, it will
give you a taste of eternity."*

BHAGWAN SHREE RAJNEESH

I had always remembered my dad smoking, whatever the occasion. Everyone's dad smoked back then. I don't remember him not smoking. He had smoked three packs of cigarettes a day for years and had tried unsuccessfully to quit smoking many times. Before bedtime one night, in the middle of winter, he was so fed up with his smoking that he took his pack of cigarettes into the backyard and buried it in the snow with a decisive "That's it, I'll never smoke again." My mother, sister and I congratulated him on his wise decision and went to bed happy in the knowledge that this time he seemed determined.

Sometime after three o'clock in the morning, we heard the wind slam the door shut. Awakened by the noise, we went into the living room. Mother opened the drapes and turned on the outside yard light. There was my father, on his hands and knees, digging in the snow for that pack of cigarettes. He was just about to light one when the light switched on and startled him. He turned and looked at our disappointed faces for what seemed like a long time, but must have only been seconds. Then he looked at the cigarette in his hand. He put it down and walked back into the house. None of us said a word. We went back to bed. My father never touched a cigarette again.

A transformation is a radical change in being. Our transformation is brought about by causes within ourselves; external causes are secondary. When we enlarge our ideas of what we can be, we create an opportunity to grow beyond our present limits.

People often ask me if this is something that takes a long time to do. In one sense, it seems to be, but in another sense, it happens instantly, immediately. When we see something clearly, we change and are liberated.

In one instant of clarity, my father saw what he was doing, and it changed him completely, forever. He saw the truth of his addiction to cigarettes, and in an instant he was liberated.

That's the way it happens. In an instant, we're liberated. But one must be willing to see the truth which liberates, and that's a problem for many people—they're not willing to see the truth.

Deep down inside we know things aren't as we think they are. And we don't like that, so we don't want to see it; we just keep covering up with beliefs. We have to see that the mind thinks it is very clear, though it never is. It may be foolish and cunning, but it is never quite as clever as it thinks it is.

People talk about wisdom, but wisdom is something that can only happen when dreaming leaves. If a person has belief systems, he is dreaming. We have to start associating beliefs with dreaming. Beliefs are dreams, they're illusions, not the truth. So wisdom can really only happen when dreaming stops and observation starts.

OBSERVING OURSELVES

"The observer is the forerunner of the Master."

—*Gurdjieff*

We begin by observing ourselves, not some great, profound truth that's out there "somewhere," but what's within ourselves. We look at what we do, objectively. By doing so, we're eventually able to clearly see what we are doing without covering it up with excuses and rationales.

We can learn more from the people who are in our lives right now than we will ever learn from some savior, avatar or old manuscript. I've observed that the simple act of dying can put a bright shine on very tarnished metal. That is less likely to happen with the living. With the living, we are faced directly with all their faults and inconsistencies.

We are revealed in the process of relationship. Compelled to seek the missing parts of ourselves, we surround ourselves with friends and mates. Separately, each of us is a fragment; life is the whole. The fragment will never be all that you want it to be. How can it be when it is only a fragment? Only when a relationship is not confined to a pattern will it give you the opportunity for self-revelation. There must be awareness without choosing one interest against another, which is the major cause of all conflict. Ever notice that the only time there is anger is when life is not going the way we want it to go, or when people are not being the way we want them to be? In other words, we only become angry when we don't get our own way.

We have to see the raw truth of who, what and where we are. That's the only way out—to go within and observe ourselves. If we continually analyze our moods, passions and fears, we are trapped within them until we can develop the ability to simply observe them, without judgment, without opinion. Only then will we be able to see clearly.

When we can do that, we're liberated. I know this because it's happened to me, and I've seen it happening in the lives of others.

We are afraid of losing our beliefs because they pacify us with the illusion of security. But they are an obstacle to the true security of self-awareness because they create an image, and images are what prevent us from seeing a thing as it actually is. If we cannot see what is real, our experience is fragmented.

We are faced with a world that is constantly changing. Would it not be more serene to embrace the flow of life instead of struggling against it? Can we allow ourselves the strength to connect with the sense of stability and vitality within us and trust our own life energy? The mere observation of the river of life transforms us from the dull, uninventive, repetitive creatures that we tend to be, into the alive creative beings that we long to become.

If you don't delude yourself with knowledge acquired by others, you can search within yourself and knowing becomes possible. We know that we are existence itself and that we are someone-who-knows—consciousness itself. (Don't handle this intellectually, just hear me out.) One part of knowing is experiencing the ecstasy, the joy of one's existence. When that is known, you will know yourself completely, even if it's only a glimpse at first.

Forget endless discussion and blame, and go deeper into an understanding of what you are now. Stop acting like a machine. Live undefined. Don't place new conditions on yourself and you will go beyond all conditioning. Spiritual maturity lies in the readiness to let everything go, realizing that there's nothing to give up because nothing is your own.

Transformation requires that we see the truth of a thing in its totality. Truth itself can only be experienced in its profound and eloquent totality; it requires awareness. We must be at the point where we desire this awareness so fully that we become willing to permit our being to go to any length to attain it.

APPROACHING THE GATEWAY

When the hunger for the full realization of who we can be leads us to enter into self-observation, we experience an expansion of the boundaries of belief that lead toward unity with the self. Developmental psychologist Pascual Leone calls what emerges from such deeply felt internal interactions the "ultraself." Transpersonal psychologist Ken Wilber describes this as the "vision-logic stage" where we become aware of "networks of relationships," or what I call the interconnectedness of life. At this stage, the beliefs of others and their different viewpoints are no longer threatening. We are able to experience true intimacy for the first time.

Developmental psychologist Charles Alexander points out that this is "the hallmark of mature adult development" where "one is said to recognize the limitations of 'closed system' formal operational reasoning that excludes sources of information that do not fit one's current worldview." He goes on to explain that such detached reflection on life "is often referred to as wisdom."

Yet many developmental psychologists agree this goal is rarely achieved. Psychologist Jane Loevinger estimates that less than 1/2 of 1 percent of the population reaches this state of wisdom. She suggests that, "theorists themselves are attempting to describe a level of which they may have some experience but lack the necessary perspective to objectively describe."

Why is it that so few reach the point where they are ready for the spontaneous leap into the unknown? Part of the answer lies in high-stress lifestyles that dilute the experience of pure consciousness and discourage detached self-observation. Alexander notes that, "until these deep stresses are fully eliminated, emotion cannot be completely life-supporting and fully integrated with cognition, nor can intuition be consistently valid." And still another part of the answer lies in the individual's willingness to grow. There is pain and effort involved in the growing process; many of us are willing to accept the fruits but not willing to do the labor. Thus progress toward the point of detached self-awareness tends to be drawn out, fragmented and incomplete.

Wilber's conclusion resonates with ancient philosophies and great spiritual traditions: "Until the unbounded value of the self, at the basis of the ego, is realized, the individual will always remain, to some extent, unfulfilled."

So we move past beliefs' boundaries into the spaciousness of freedom where we begin to know who we are but have yet to learn who we might become. We tremble on the edge of the communion that will connect the realms of essence and existence, and complete our reality. As Dorothy said in *The Wizard of Oz*, "I don't think we're in Kansas anymore, Toto."

PASSING THROUGH DISILLUSIONMENT

To begin the process, we must be willing to remove the blinders of beliefs at all costs. It's not an easy path. When we question these illusions and tenets, we pass through the distress of disillusionment.

Disillusionment can prepare us for the next step. When we become completely disillusioned with the person we have been and the life we have been leading, we've completed almost half the journey. I think disillusionment is one of the greatest things that can ever happen to a person. When people stop being complacent and self-satisfied with who they are, they are able to see themselves clearly— maybe for the very first time. Disillusionment opens many doors because when people doubt, they begin to question their values, traditions, ideals, illusions ... their beliefs. And at this point, they are able to move beyond the illusions that get in the way of their becoming all that they can be.

True understanding requires that you begin to doubt the firm beliefs you hold, especially those pertaining to religion, God, and the true meaning of life. Many people believe it's not good to doubt or be disillusioned, but in order to reach the point of true understanding and awareness, it is necessary. When you really desire to become consciously aware, you are no longer able to blindly accept things the way you once did. You begin to release the security of the familiar fantasy for the knowledge of reality. So people who want to live more fully need to doubt the belief they most love, even the very thing you are pursuing. You can't blindly accept anything. When you're doubting, that means that you are trying to discover something. In order to do that you have to let go of the things that you hold so close to you.

You can't hold on to something and examine it at the same time. You have to release it so you can see it completely. That's what doubt and disillusionment accomplish—the ability to finally relinquish the tight hold we've had on our beliefs and take a good, hard look at them. And that's what observation is. It's the ability to really be in a sense detached. Even just for a little while from something, so that you can see.

• *What about faith?*

After all this talk of doubt and disillusionment, I can hear some of you asking, "But what about faith?" Blind belief is what you must question. Faith is not blind. Faith alone, however, is not enough but must be expressed in action: it is the willingness to try. To be alert and watchful is to have faith in yourself. Faith is a quality whereas belief is a concept. Those who are afraid cling to their beliefs and try to convince, coerce or force others into agreeing with them to achieve validation. It's that old idea that if a lot of people agree on something, it must be true. I say that's absurd. Truth is truth, no matter how many people agree or disagree with it. Quality is important, not quantity. Faith has its place and serves us, but we're talking about knowing. If you don't know a thing, having faith in it will only give you the experience you hoped for and not the real. It's far more valuable to see clearly that you don't know. Beliefs are beliefs, period, and will keep us in a perpetual dream state unless they are utilized only when needed and then relinquished as soon as possible.

LETTING GO

The awesome experience of opening to reality will give you everything while simultaneously taking everything away—no more hiding in the illusion of your beliefs. In a sense, it resembles death, which is why it is frequently referred to as "dying to self." It's a complete release of everything. In this process we're dying every day to what we know. And to die to everything—all your knowledge and beliefs—is the beginning of wisdom.

While transformation happens in an instant, awakening is not a single experience—it is a process that unfolds in its own timing on many levels. It is a never-ending process, something that you do from moment to moment. It's never finished.

What happens is you're constantly refreshed. Your body, mind and spirit are continually renewed because every day is something different. You're no longer living with preconceived notions and beliefs. You're open and available to all life has to offer. What a tremendous reward! The wonderful thing is that all you need do is release, you don't have to add anything. People think that if they let something go, they have to add something else because the emptiness makes them nervous. That's the reconditioning reflex.

When I am inside the void, I can feel the One Power. There is nothing but me and the power—thought and emotion remain outside. I used to take it a little at a time, but all the beauty and life and wonderment comes at once now. I surrender to it, and by surrendering, I can direct it, if appropriate.

This emptiness is really the highest form of love, as far as I'm concerned, because there's no reactive memory, no conclusions that distort perception and blind us to what is. The joy that people seek comes at the moment of emptiness. When your mind isn't cluttered with things, it has a chance to be silent. It becomes clear and pristine. The mind moves beyond pleasure to joyousness, independent of external factors.

WORDLESSNESS

Existence is nameless. As long as no name is given, everything is One. With words there is no way to escape duality. Words are a contrivance for those who understand only the language of words; they can create a terrible block to awareness because when we name something, we no longer see it for what it really is, we only see the symbol or label we have placed on it. We separate it from the rest and make it an object. When we speak, we bring in duality; it is impossible not to. Obviously, when we wish to convey something to another person, we usually make use of words, but there is no need to use words simply for one's self. If we constantly listen to the inner "babbler," so many words pile up within us that we completely lose sight of our inner mystery. Only when these superficial layers of words are removed can we become acquainted with that center.

Pluck a guitar string and listen to how the resonance of the note begins to fade. Can you hear where the resonance gradually lost itself in non-resonance? In much the same way, words slowly merge into silence. The full and empty define each other.

It is in the silent spaces that we find definition, just as it is the intervals in music that allow us to hear the melody, and the relationship of light and dark that enable us to see.

In the same way that sound is a vibration of sound and silence, the entire universe—all of existence—is a vibration of solids and spaces. When we move our attention from the conscious thinking level that uses words (the solids) through higher levels of consciousness, the mind arrives at the "spaces" of pure awareness.

When we have refocused our attention past the noise and confusion of the "babbler" in our minds, we become aware of the quiet of "no-mind." It is in the silence of "no-mind" that we transcend the limitations of ordinary perception and hear the melody of the soul. We are able to experience periods of wordlessness in which we are able to see things clearly. Buddha said, "Whatever I say is not to tell you of That Which Is, rather it is to lead you there."

Obviously, I have a thing about words. For instance, people in my seminars ask why I don't talk more about love. I respond by saying that everything I talk about concerns love, but they wanted to hear the word itself. They don't understand that the word conjures up all the concepts and beliefs they hold about love.

Another example of a concept-laden word is "God." When people hear the word "God," it triggers their belief systems and they no longer are capable of thinking clearly. Their beliefs enable them to set aside the reality in favor of the concept. You believe a certain thing about a person or group of people, such as Asians, homosexuals, fundamentalists, or women, and it enables you to dismiss them. It's a prejudice, which is also a loaded word.

Most people deny their prejudice because the word has developed such negative connotations, usually relating to racial issues, when all the word "prejudice" means is "a preconceived judgment or opinion."

Here's a thought I'd like to spring on you—*all* beliefs are prejudices. Makes you stop and think, doesn't it?

RELEASE OF ENERGY

Can you imagine the tremendous energy that is at your disposal when you release your prejudices? Beliefs and illusions aren't maintenance-free; because they are conflicts and cause suppression, they use tremendous amounts of energy. On the other hand, no energy is required to release them. Once released, that energy then becomes available for use in other areas of your life.

Fletcher was a young man who came to me complaining of a lack of aliveness in his life. After we talked about what was happening (or not happening) in his life, I told him to let go of his ideas about his parents. He had a lot of childhood issues relating to his parents and had nurtured negative ideas about them for years. Now he wondered why he felt so tired and uninvolved in life. He finally understood that these ideas arising out of old programming were using up all his energy. I would estimate eighty percent of his attitude toward his parents was negative, only twenty percent positive. Rather than telling him to concentrate on the twenty percent positive feelings, I told him to release

all the feelings, positive and negative. The complete disappearance of resistance, for and against, would free one hundred percent of his energy and allow him to move into a completely new state.

ENTERING INTO FREEDOM

It's so simple. It doesn't start a month from now when you're prepared or six weeks from now or a year from now. It starts right now, while you are reading this book. It's like telling someone not to think about a pink elephant. Once the idea of transcending beliefs is planted, you immediately begin to observe your process. It's irrepressible.

People think that freedom is something that they are going to attain at the end of some process. Not true. It doesn't come at the end, it comes at the beginning. You have to become free first, then that liberation allows you to see everything in your life more clearly. Discovery is impossible without freedom. There can't be any compromise. Freedom is freedom. If you're going to be free, you're either free of everything or you're not free at all. You can't be a little bit free.

7

THE NEXT STEP: SET YOURSELF FREE

"Man is just a bridge between two eternities, the eternity of nature and the eternity of God."

FRIEDRICH NIETZSCHE

Human consciousness is a most mysterious reality to experience. Many think that it is something that happens to you, that it cannot be sought. This impression is inaccurate; a fully developed consciousness is both an active and a productive state of mind.

More than ever before, it is time to be as present as possible. We must see and accept what is here and now if we are ever to unveil the illusions which surround us and reveal the profound mystery of existence within ourselves. It is not far away in some past or future life. It will not be revealed through some master being. Leave these things. Leave all you think you know. Enter into existence now, this very moment.

Existence has never been far away. It is not a place that is to be reached. It is closer than near. It is simple, ordinary and exists in the profoundly mundane. Unless we let go of the far away, the conceptual and the burdensome knowledge that has enslaved us and come back to the here and now, we are doomed to continue in this perpetual dream state from which all life's misery flows. The sooner you become aware and drop out of the philosophy trap, the better, because life will not wait for you and your theories.

You are the adventure: discover and live this truth now. It happens right here, right now—in fact, that's the only way it happens ... if you will only allow it.

LIVING HONESTLY

My car came to a stop at a crowded intersection. It was late afternoon, hot and noisy. I was tired and anxious to get home. Glancing out the window, I saw a homeless man sitting on the curb. He wore a sign with the word "Hungry" on it. Next to him stood an enthusiastic young man holding out plastic bags of fruit—grapes in one bag, oranges in another. He also had a sign. It read "Fresh fruit, $1 a bag." The scene was so bizarre I wished I'd had a camera. I could have sold it to *Life* magazine.

Life is a wild thing, full of irony and inconsistency; it's unpredictable and uncompromising. The incredible beauty and adventure of life lies in its ability to always be a surprise, and you can't be surprised if you have specific beliefs about it. You can only be disappointed. Experience the joy and richness of life by allowing yourself to be both earthly and unearthly. Since it's possible to be both, why miss out on anything? Use every opportunity to grow and to be. Life is a force, a power, an energy. Life soars. Meet life on its terms and you will soar with it. Let the roots of your earthly experiences grow deep and varied, and you will reach higher than you've ever dreamed possible because you will be more complete.

Don't let anyone impose on you his beliefs about what is wrong with you. The ego may need to be transformed, it's true, but not because it's wrong or bad or evil. It simply has to be observed; what is meaningless will start fading away of its own accord, while what is meaningful will begin to materialize and grow. The beauty in being watchful is not that we have to work to bring about its transformation but that life itself—the Whole—transforms it.

All existence is beautiful. There is nowhere to hide from it. Just remember that if you live totally, honestly, truthfully, things may begin to go deeper. When things are deepening, they begin to change. Accept the feeling of insecurity this may bring, and trust your energy. Don't compromise; there's no need to—insecurity will disappear without compromise on your part.

Be careful not to destroy today by being afraid of tomorrow, because if today has been destroyed, where will tomorrow come from? If you don't worry about what tomorrow will bring, and if you accept tomorrow's insecurity, you will live today so courageously that a beautiful tomorrow will arise out of that totality. So while you are alive, **be alive!** Don't concern yourself with how long it lasts.

THE NEXT STEP

The next step surpasses all the steps of ordinary consciousness. Transformation is instantaneous, not gradual. Reality is what makes the present so vital. The real is always with you. You don't have to wait for what you are.

The ordinary, common mind that is part of the human condition has a built-in need to have its beliefs verified by others who believe similarly. The common mind automatically seeks out and finds this confirmation for its own comfort and security. To surround itself with others who have the same wants and needs, who will support and perpetuate one another's dreaming, so that it will stay comfortably incarcerated within the framework of its delusions, is the common and habitual thing to do. This is not a criticism; it is to be expected while dwelling in ordinary consciousness (herd mentality) because that is exactly what we are supposed to do, or more accurately "must do," while in that generic state.

There is also the uncommon mind—the God or spiritual mind. If you have reached a point where you have the capacity (if not always the willingness) to enter into a very different state of consciousness—a place that has nothing to do with ordinary consciousness—you are, in a sense, alone. You will find there are few books you can read and even fewer places you can go that will support you or offer any confirmation of this extraordinary state. You begin to realize how completely mechanical you have been and how predictable this world and everyone in it is. At this point, you will find it increasingly difficult to express your experience of this state and virtually impossible to follow the herd just for the comfort it provides. Because, in contrast to this extraordinary state, herd consciousness is always mundane, unremarkable, unoriginal and dulling.

In this step there is a different quality of hearing and seeing that is truly significant and very uncommon. It is, in fact, extremely rare, although at first glance it will appear not to be. It will, at first hearing, sound ordinary. That's because you are listening with your ordinary consciousness. This vital step is the ability to hear what you **need** to hear, not what you **want** to hear.

RESISTANCE TO CHANGE

If you're not able to hear what you need to hear, you will continually seek out places in which to encounter what you already know. You will hold onto what you want to be true about yourself, God, love, life and the world. You won't go anywhere or listen for very long to anyone who may disturb that illusion. You will, once again, need to be disillusioned. It's the only way to incite your consciousness to move within a system that is so ponderous and mechanically repetitive.

This pattern must be broken because it affects every single area of your life and is the major obstacle to going beyond ordinary consciousness. You must see that this is indeed what you do and then face up to the possibility that things may not be what you want them to be. Would you be willing to hear that? Could you hear it?

The next step is tricky because the dominant part of you will assert that, "I *am* open to hearing what I need to hear!" That is definitely not true. You will deny this; you will become defensive and argue that you are open and available. (You're probably doing so right now.) Ask yourself if you are prepared to hear something new, something which you may not like, or, are you prepared to hear only that which you already know and/or that which you want to believe?

When hearing something new, this dominant part of yourself will say, "Even if what you say is true, I don't like it!" If you don't like something, you'll never see it. You won't believe it, you won't trust it—you will simply reject it. However, your opinion has no bearing on the fact that ordinary consciousness simply does not want to hear anything new. It wants to hear what it wants to hear; when it catches a glimpse of what it *needs* to hear, ordinary consciousness blocks this information because it doesn't really want to hear it.

If you have the capacity to look at this, here is what you need to consider now. Don't think that your consciousness is extraordinary because you regard yourself as a "spiritual" person, accumulate volumes of metaphysical, occult and ancient knowledge, have met extraterrestrials, can read the stars or speak with the dead. That's all a diversion and of no consequence as far as awakening is concerned.

When you have gone to the extreme polarity of what your ordinary consciousness calls "spiritual," this prominent part becomes especially deceptive. Its allure is its ability to make the mundane appear to be "new," unusual, interesting and fun. This is actually a ruse to keep you involved and under its mechanical influence so you will feel as though you have transcended it.

Resistance to change is inherent on the level of the mechanical structure of your ordinary consciousness. You want to hear what you want to hear from what ordinary consciousness sees as a new and exciting source. But it's important to see that what you are capable of hearing at the ordinary level is what you have already heard, what reinforces the beliefs of your conventional consciousness. The "exotic" is not telling you anything new. It's keeping you where you are ... in the grip of the ordinary.

THE BRIDGE

At the beginning of this chapter is a quote from Nietzsche. It bears repeating: "Man is just a bridge between two eternities, the eternity of nature and the eternity of

God." Keep in mind that eternity is not a duration of time. Eternity exists in the here and now, this present moment.

Nature exists in eternity, as does God, functioning appropriately from moment to moment. As I write this, my house is swaying back and forth from one of the thousands of aftershocks Los Angeles is experiencing after a major earthquake. I know that at this moment, people throughout the city are experiencing fear as they feel the tremor. But the earth is doing what it has done for millennia. It doesn't have a problem with that—it is alive and ever transforming itself.

Man, however, lives in time. He takes natural occurrences personally and gives them human attributes, such as a "vicious" storm, an "angry" earthquake. He calls an unknowable God "loving" or "wrathful," depending on what suits his purpose. This is because man is in the middle—he is half-nature and half-God, and doesn't know what to make of it. He is confused and ever striving to be certain, but you can only be certain if you don't know much. The more you know, the more confused you become. You can never be certain if you know a lot, and there is no clarity in one who knows little and is therefore certain, because they are simply unaware of contradictory facts which could confuse them. Only the ignorant can be certain. When a person becomes more aware, more present, the mind diminishes, and all uncertainty *and* certainty diminish along with it.

Problems result from the way man looks at the world. Because man has a divided consciousness, it distorts his perception. He sees "two" where there is only "one."

Whenever there are "two," there is conflict.

Some people lean more toward the common part of their mind, others toward their "God" side. The difference between a mind that is spiritual and one that is common is that a common mind thinks, "There is nothing wrong with me—everything else is wrong." Common-minded people take no responsibility; blame is always placed elsewhere. "Things will be just fine if they go the way I think they should go." So they constantly try to change the world around them. But is there any more happiness in the world as the result of these efforts?

DOING VERSUS BEING

As you move through the phases of becoming more aware, it may sometimes appear as if nothing is happening. You are so accustomed to effort that just **being** is very unsettling. You desire outer activity because you are not used to taking the time to look at the reality of what is happening to you. In allowing yourself to simply **be**, you may feel insufficient as you are, so you become unsettled. See that you are feeling unsettled and be with that feeling. Settle into being unsettled. Remember: Nothing is lacking and there is no excess. Everything is balanced. *You* are the problem, not the world around you.

When you observe a flower, do you think nothing is happening? Just because you are not sensitive to the flower doesn't mean nothing is happening. If you are completely present with the flower, you will sense that it is a living happening—alive, sensitive to the sun and wind, pulsating with life. How silly to expect it to do something, as if simply existing were not enough. Can you see how silly the demands you place on yourself are?

When you think nothing is going on with you, it is because you lack sensitivity. Sensitivity requires availability, vulnerability and observation. It may take time for you to adjust to this pace because you are used to running so fast.

Non-doing is difficult. The mind wants something to practice, but practice is not necessary. Enlightenment can happen in an instant. It is not a question of how to bring it about but how to allow it. You know something so profound is taking place deep within yourself that it cannot be analyzed or explained; words are inadequate.

When the inessential has been released, the essential is revealed. A magnificent simplicity of being is born. You become ordinary; to be ordinary is the most extraordinary thing in the world. Others are striving to be extraordinary, which makes their pursuit the most ordinary of all.

I'll address some common questions, then offer you some techniques that will help you in the process of awareness.

• *Is there a technique I can use to know the truth?*

Don't try to know the truth, just know what is not true. That's enough to free you from the false. What I'm about to tell you is not a technique—just be available to the sense of it.

Non-investigation is the main cause of bondage. When you don't know, you are free to investigate. If you are listening to me and something awakens within you, you will have an insight—something will be sensed, perceived. I'm not trying to convince you. I'm just conveying a fact to you. The only preparation for it, in a sense, is that you must not be identified with your knowledge, your beliefs. I mean prepared in the sense that you understand the meaninglessness of everything you have ever known.

It is your awareness of the thinking process, an awareness that can move you into a place where a realization of *what is* can occur. It's called an awakening, a realization, or an insight. I sometimes refer to it as "the happening."

• *How do we go beyond our belief systems?*

Investigate. A thing recognized is a thing transcended. Observation effortlessly produces its own change. Whatever needs to remain will; the rest will fall away.

What's difficult is that we've enmeshed ourselves in so much fantasy that separating the real from fantasy can be very challenging. But it is possible and worth the effort, or I would not have written this book.

• *Why is it so difficult to let go?*

People don't want to let go of anything because they're afraid they'll be left with nothing. They think that to let go means to get rid of something. Letting go is more like going to sleep. You don't give up your bed when you fall asleep; you just forget it. Not understanding this, they are afraid and consequently, seek to substitute one belief for another, one form of conditioning for another and they call that freedom. They don't know that the finite is the price of the infinite, just as death is the price of immortality.

- *Is it possible for me to observe everything around me in my daily life without the shadow of images or beliefs?*

In time, yes. Not at first perhaps, but you must begin now, right where you are, this very minute, and you must find out for yourself. Don't take my word for it. Don't believe me. Awareness or perception implies a state of seeing in which there is no image. There is the experience of just being.

- *What is the witnessing that you encourage?*

Inside the body there appears to be an observer and outside—a world under observation. The witnessing I encourage is in itself a meditation, a living process of being available and non-resistant to what comes uninvited. Witnessing is the last remnant of illusion, the first touch of the real. Beyond it all, there is the unknown, some call it God. This crossover I call the Gap.

- *How is the Gap created?*

It already exists. There is no need to create it by believing in it. The Gap (void, silence, space, God) created by your mind will not be real, it will just be your own creation. In order to enter the void, (the Oneness), belief and thought must cease.

- *What about certain diets or behavior? Do they help us become more aware?*

Outer circumstances can either help or hinder inner circumstances, but cannot change them. A situation can be created by outer circumstances so that the inner can erupt more easily, but outer transformation is not inner transformation.

The efforts you make on the outside must not become a substitute for inner transformation. The outer you will never feel ready to transform because it has decided on certain qualifications and preconceived specifications that must be fulfilled before it will be ready. But it will never be ready. Obsessions with the kind of food you eat, the clothes you wear, or certain behavior can be hindrances. I'm not saying to neglect them, because they can be helpful, but be aware that the inner you is not touched by them. The outer is the extremity while the inner is the central part of yourself. Don't use activity on the outside to escape what is needed inside.

• *Am I responsible for everything that happens?*

Shifting responsibility is a uniquely human game. You're responsible only for what you can change, and you can only change yourself. Realizing this is the first step.

At one level, you must clearly see and take full responsibility in order to affect any transformation in your distorted way of seeing. Then, and only then, can you transcend responsibility.

You will see the belief that a particular thing can cause an event is incorrect. For anything to happen, the entire universe must consent. Every cause is universal. Your body would not exist without the entire universe contributing to its creation and survival. To affect the course of events, you must bring a new element into the world and that element can only be you, the power of love and understanding focused on yourself.

TECHNIQUES

I will offer some techniques you may find helpful in the beginning, but be aware that they too must be transcended. Use them and be willing to release them or they will become an addiction. Addictions medicate pain. Unless the pain is seen, the addiction remains. Consciousness is a flow from past to future—awareness happens only in the present.

LOVE EXERCISE

Do this exercise everywhere. Be aware of the energy radiating from your body but don't direct it. Try to sense it. When I say "sense" it, I don't mean emotionally. Sensing something is not the same as feeling something. Allow the energy to be absorbed by whomever or whatever needs it. Don't interfere, just let it radiate from you, without focusing on a a particular object.

In love, all fear disappears. There is no tomorrow, there is no past. This moment is enough. Love just is—you can't do anything about it. If you do, it becomes artificial.

THE "I DON'T KNOW" EXERCISE

All day, be aware of everything you say. Whenever you find yourself coming to conclusions about anything, ask yourself "What do I really know about it?"

In this exercise, you must stay especially alert to hear your own opinions. Actually, it's kind of fun to catch yourself in the act. Remember not to change anything, just be aware. You may be surprised at how many conclusions you reach.

MOTIVE EXERCISE

The One Power is responsive to our intentions and expectations. Our expectations cause the energy we channel through us to affect other energies. Spend a day concentrating on "why." Know *why* you do what you do and be honest about it. Don't discuss your reasons with anyone, just be aware of your real motives.

NO EXPLANATION EXERCISE

Spend the day not explaining any of your actions. Even if you are asked, just say, "I have my reasons." It takes a certain amount of courage to do this because we usually feel that we are expected to explain everything we do—especially if we say no to someone. Can you not explain yourself for one day?

THANKFULNESS EXERCISE

Thankfulness is loaded with energy. Begin to appreciate everything. Realize that you don't know what current experiences will mean to you in the future. Be thankful all day for everything that happens or doesn't happen.

THE STOP EXERCISE

The name of this exercise tells you what it's all about. It's quite simple—all you have to do is just stop. Stop. Observe what you're feeling, what you're doing, what you're thinking. Take a moment and just be aware, be present.

THE AUTOMOBILE EXERCISE

You can modify the **Stop Exercise** for use in the car. Now, obviously, you don't want to completely stop the car unless you're parking. I call this modified version the **Automobile Exercise**. Just before you get in the car, take a deep breath. Stop yourself and be aware of what you're doing. Get in your car and set off on your trip, but instead of driving on autopilot, thinking about what you're going to do later, slow down and take a good look at your surroundings. If you're going 90 miles an hour, it's not very easy to observe because you're too busy handling the car. The slower you go, the more you see. Be aware of everything you're passing. If you're traveling a familiar route, be aware that it's not the same. Things are different. Flowers have grown, trees have changed, different people and cars are on the sidewalks and roads. It's like a kaleidoscope—every day, different colors, shapes and patterns. We take this for granted because we're lost in our thoughts. Slow down.

You can also apply the **Automobile Exercise** to walking. While walking, pause now and then. Slow down and be aware of the physical feeling of walking. Be aware of your muscles stretching, the air flowing past your face, the sights and sounds around you. Don't try and change anything or improve on anything. Look. See. Be totally there.

OBSERVATION AND AWARENESS

Acceptance is not a state of inaction or passivity. It is the first step to successful action. You relax, you let go, you are patient and peaceful. In this state you merely are. In this state there are no expectations. There is no unnecessary doing. When you are calm, detached and in complete acceptance, you see the truth of a thing. Then truth acts. This action is different in that it is much more effective than if you try to do something based on your beliefs about what should be done.

This exercise has to do with being quiet. Sit down in a comfortable position and take a deep breath, which slows the body's system and helps you observe more about yourself. Begin observing your body. The body is the easiest thing to observe, and the easiest to feel separate from. Be aware of the sensations your body is feeling. If you feel uncomfortable, see if you can be with that feeling. If you must move, be aware that you're moving. If you judge the fact that you can't sit in one position, go ahead and judge. Be aware that you're judging the fact that you're judging. Being constantly aware allows your body to be whatever it is.

When you've done this for a while and feel ready to move on to another area, explore listening. Listen, really listen to all the sounds around you and see how many you can pick up. You'll hear things you may not have noticed before—a dog barking in the distance, the hum of traffic, birds or the wind. Listen to all the sounds you normally don't hear because you're so preoccupied.

When you've exhausted that area, move to your feelings. Be aware of what feelings are happening. Don't worry about judgment right now. Judgment is of the mind; just observe that. So, be aware of all your feelings without judgment. If you do find yourself judging them as good or bad feelings, then be aware that it is your mind judging. That's what minds do—they judge. If you're having a sad or unhappy feeling, see if you can leave it alone and be with it. Try not to push it away or exchange it for any other feeling. Take time and be aware of every feeling that you're having at the moment. Don't conjure anything, just experience what you are experiencing.

Move on to your thoughts. Watch them as they come and go. Be like the sky and let the thoughts be like clouds, coming and going of their own accord. Observe all this.

This exercise leads to your becoming more aware in every aspect of your life. You will be aware of the times you restrict yourself, when you want to say or do something and don't, when you shut down. You'll become more aware of your expansive moments when you are in tune with everything around you. Be aware, don't judge, let these things just occur naturally. Be aware of every moment. See if you can spend a period of time not improving yourself. Just watch. Soon, you'll get to a point where you'll find yourself automatically observing yourself, the world, and everything in it. This is the habit of awareness. It's a little different from complete awareness. Eventually, you drop even the habit of awareness and just live in pure awareness. You will be aware and not have the need to express it, explain it, or be understood. You won't need any of these things. You will no longer need to be right. You will no longer need to be agreed with. All these things will fall by the wayside. You'll simply be aware.

I would like to stress that when you are observing the body, anything you observe is not you. If you can observe the body, then you are not the body. If you can observe feelings, then you are not the feelings. If you can observe the mind, you are not the mind. Then what's watching all of this?

"WHAT IS PERMANENT IN YOU" EXERCISE

No matter what you have experienced in your life, there is something about you that has never changed or been affected in any way. What is that something? **Do not name it**—don't call it your "higher self," or "God," or the "soul" because that will separate you from it. Don't call it anything. Don't believe in it, just sense it. The sense of it will come and go; let it—you cannot hold onto that either. You can only discover this for yourself. How?

Watch! Watch everything. Observe it all as it happens, then ask yourself, "Who is watching this pain, this fear, this body, these emotions?" Anything you can watch and observe is not you! This, unfortunately, cannot be fully explained, which is frustrating for me at times. It's not in the words. Just try to get the **sense** of what I am saying. Watch.

THE SKY TECHNIQUE

In order for this technique to be clear, you must first try to understand the structure of the mind. You cannot *make* the mind clear. It cannot be whipped into submission, as so many techniques and groups attempt to do. The mind can be left behind, dropped, but it will never be clear—that is impossible. It is the mind's nature to be full of concepts and belief—"stuff." Mind is a continuous process of thoughts gathered from everywhere, like a storeroom full of things you think you may need someday. Of course, for the most part, you never will, which is why these things were stored in the first place. So they go on collecting dust. All confusion is stored in the mind. Drop the mind and confusion is dropped, but first it must be understood.

Think of it this way. Your awareness is like a clear blue sky while your mind is like a cluster of clouds. The sky is not affected by the clouds, which come and go as they will. The sky remains clear.

When flying in an airplane, there is always turbulence at takeoff, especially as you pass through a cloud layer. Once you break through, however, you level off and everything is smooth and peaceful. The clouds are below you now and you may think, "Ah, the sun has come out." But the sun was always shining. You don't need to change the clouds to enter the clarity of the sky; just see the clouds as clouds and go past them. That's where peace is, higher in consciousness.

So here is the exercise: On the next clear day, preferably early or late in the day when the sun is not too bright, meditate on the empty sky. No clouds, no birds, no planes. Stare at the sky without blinking. Meditate on this pristine sky and enter into its clarity. Become one with it.

You will begin to feel the mind disappearing. There will be gaps as the mind begins to drop away, and you will begin to be aware that the clear sky has entered into you. There will be only moments of clarity at first, but these intervals will begin to lengthen as the clouds within you begin to dissipate. Your thoughts will get out of the way, and the outer clarity will become one with the inner. They are already one; it has only been the constant thoughts (cloud cover) which made a barrier. The sky doesn't begin at some point above the earth; it is the same sky one foot above the ground as at thirty thousand feet above.

The sky has no boundaries. This helps your boundaries disappear because this open sky will be reflected within you. Stare into that emptiness and feel that you have become one with it. If you can do this, even for a moment, you will experience realization because in that moment there is no mind. You are not thinking, and that is the only time realization can happen. There is no fear; there is only the present, because the past and the future belong to the mind. Existence *is* the present.

Remember these things: 1) Don't blink; just stare, even if it is uncomfortable. If you blink, your thoughts will continue. Let your eyes tear up and let them unload the tears.

2) Don't *think* about the sky. Do not think *about* it. Simply enter it, be one with it, or you will create another barrier. If you move into the sky, it will immediately move into you. Take your time or it's not effective, but don't think of time. Just let yourself be lost in the sky. Then, when you really feel that you have become one with the sky, you can close your eyes and you will see it within also.

3) After you feel that you and the sky have become one, enter that clarity. Don't say anything, just feel it. You will know when. Just be aware of the clarity all around and within you. You are not to imagine any of this. It's not necessary; the clarity is already there.

4) Remember to be vulnerable. Nothing can enter you

without your allowing yourself to be vulnerable to it. Don't project it; allow it to happen. Don't force it.

YES EXERCISE

Spend a day saying yes to everything. "Yes" is open and available and lets your energy flow freely. "No" stops your energy, and usually comes out of fear and mistrust. There is a strong tendency to stop the flow and remain in control by saying no, thereby resisting life so nothing can happen. Growth becomes sluggish. Embrace the life force that flows from everything and that life embraces you. Trust that all will work out. Just say "yes."

BELIEF ANALYSIS EXERCISE

To begin to really understand what you believe and why, write down your beliefs. The physical act of writing is important because there is a certain clarity that occurs as a result. Get a nice big notebook with lots of pages in it because you are going to discover that you have many more beliefs than you realize.

- *#1: What do I believe (or disbelieve) in?*
  (Disbelief is also a belief).

Begin with "What do I believe?" Remember to include the beliefs you have when you watch television or read the newspapers. Write down as many as you can, and leave plenty of room for the beliefs you'll become aware of later on.

- *#2: Where did I acquire this belief?*

What is the source of this belief? Did it come from my

parents, teachers, a friend; my church or religious teaching; a book, newspaper or tabloid, television or movies? Put some thought into this one and you may be surprised at what you come up with.

- ### #3: What do I really know about it?

The key to this step is not what you *believe* you know, but what the facts are that support the belief. If it's a belief, you may not know too many facts about it, but see what you come up with, then question those as well. Keep in mind that if you believe in a book, let's use the Bible for an example, then you must realize that your *belief* that the Bible is the word of God forms the basis for other beliefs you hold.

- ### #4: Why do I believe this?

Why *do* you believe it? This is extremely important. Is it because it fits in with the way you want, or hope things are, or will be? Is it because you feel empowered or special by having this belief? Is it because your ego is enhanced as a result of believing this? Are you afraid not to?

It is of utmost importance that you are honest with yourself. If you cannot be truthful with yourself, you'll never be truthful with anyone else.

Here is an excerpt of a conversation I had with an audience member during a talk I gave several years ago. This is basically the conversation you need to have with yourself while you are doing the **Belief Analysis Exercise.**

"Usually speakers talk a lot about love, but I've noticed that you don't mention love or God very often.

Why is that?"

"I don't use the words 'love' and 'God' very often because they cause the mind to project too much of what one *wants* them to be. This leaves no room for experiencing what *is*. All this incessant talk of love! If we really loved, we wouldn't have to talk about it so much."

"I worship and love God."

"Why?"

"What do you mean?"

"Why do you worship God?"

"Because I love him."

"Why do you love 'him'?"

"Because I do!" (An uncomfortable laugh, followed by a long pause.) **"I don't know ... because I love him. Isn't that reason enough?"**

"Reason enough for a person who never took the time to explore, or reason enough for one who has been told he should? What do you think would happen if you didn't love God?"

"I don't know. Probably something bad. I'd get struck by lightning or something."

"You don't love God; you're afraid of him. Your heart is full of fear, not love, and this is what is important for you to see. Churches, temples and sacred things are not of God; they are the creations of our vanity and fear. Only the unhappy and frightened worship God. If you put aside these things and understand *why* you are unhappy instead of enveloping yourself in the refuge of your belief *about* God, you'll experience the truth of God."

"I guess that frightens me."

"One of the greatest fears is of releasing one's concept of God. Your 'god' has to conform to your distorted idea of him because if he doesn't, you won't detect him at all. You insist on your idea of particulars. Goddesses are the current trap. Don't let your fear of God prevent you from exploring the truth. Don't use God to escape. Watch these pretensions and drop them. If you really want to be an authentic person, be true to yourself."

"How do I do that?"

"If you haven't loved, face the fact and know it. Drop all the illusions and remain true to your being, whatever it may be. Since it is not possible to know yourself through another, no matter how great he may be, you must know yourself directly. Then many things become possible."

"What would there be left to believe in, then?"

"Why believe at all? Isn't nature enough? It's so much more rewarding and creative. Is it because you don't trust nature or the universe? You *are* nature itself *and* the universe, but you don't trust your own life energy. If you can't trust your own life energy, you'll never trust another's. This is obvious when you look at the state of the world.

"If we look through our own little belief system, we can't see what's really happening in our world. Seeing is understanding, and we cannot understand through the mind, which is only a fragment. Understanding happens when the mind is quiet."

"What do you mean by 'quiet'?"

"By quiet, I mean no images."

"What about unconditional love?"

135

"Start by seeing *yourself* clearly, that is to say, unconditionally. This act of seeing is an act of love because it is unconditional, untainted. Only love makes the mind sensitive. This seeing, observing and listening are the greatest acts. If you want to be free and unconditional, start by exploring your beliefs and releasing all that is binding you. You cannot love unconditionally with beliefs that, by their very nature, have boundaries."

MEDITATION

Reports of transcendental experiences throughout history show a striking similarity that cuts across cultural, social and intellectual distinctions. Researchers have found fundamental, universally available conditions that are present in these experiences.

Hundreds of studies of meditators show that "repeated experience of pure consciousness during meditation produces significantly greater reductions in trait anxiety, depression, hostility and other symptoms of mental stress than [experienced during] simple or stylized forms of relaxation." This research is very careful to separate the practice of meditation from the experiences of pure consciousness. Although the practice is helpful, it is the experience of transcendence itself that is of the greatest benefit.

Listen to the language of a scientist discussing quantum physics—it sounds remarkably like the language of the soul; one becomes aware that physics and metaphysics can be thought of as two sides of the same coin. The metaphors of metaphysics are simply attempts to describe what we are as yet unable to perceive with any stability. Those who have fully experienced the state of transcendence are termed "mystics" who "understand our logic." We cannot fathom the more unified, yet seemingly paradoxical, nature of their cognitions until we too become transcendent. You can't get away from the fact. You've got to be there to understand it.

MEDITATION TECHNIQUES

Meditation is many things to many people, depending on culture, religious traditions, psychological orientation, the individual's purpose, etc. Whatever, it is not the definition but the experience that matters.

Meditation opens the doors of perception, integrating the mind and body, the aim being to refocus attention past the noise and confusion of the "babbler" in our minds. When this happens, we become aware of the quiet of "no-mind," a state of pure consciousness with no content.

There is also a body of scientific research showing that meditation is more effective in the alleviation of anxiety than therapy. Meditators have been shown in a recent, large-scale "meta-analysis" (a statistical technique designed to compare research across a variety of studies) to be significantly more self-actualized than psychotherapy patients. In addition, surprising things like prison recidivism are significantly lower for prisoners who meditate than for those who go into therapy.

Traditionally associated with Eastern religions, meditation has been practiced in one form or another in all religions and in most societies. Meditation researcher Michael West notes that:

American Indians practice a form of meditation remarkably similar to zazen [Zen meditation]. In Africa, in the Kalahari Desert, the people of the !Kung Zhu/twasi practice a form of ritual dancing (like Islamic Sufi dancing) which activates a postulated energy source and produces an 'ecstasy' experience. Many tribal groups practice such ritual dancing coupled with chanting to produce altered states of consciousness. ... The Eskimo would sit facing a large soft stone and using a small, hard hand-stone, would carve a circle in the large stone continuously to produce trance. Meditation has long been used within the Christian religion and many of the Christian techniques are identical to those used in other religions, cultures, and times.

Basically, there are two forms of meditation: **active** and **silent**. Historically, active forms have used chanting, drums, dancing and music to produce altered states of consciousness. Silent forms of meditation use four techniques to access pure consciousness: **concentration, contemplation, mental repetition of a sound,** and **detached observation.**

Since the subject matter covers a large body of work, I'll give a very brief overview. You may obtain books at your local library or bookstore that will go into more detail.

- Concentration of a steadily visualized image or symbol, such as a mystical rose, a thousand-petalled lotus, a crescent moon, or Star of David; focus on the breath; concentrate on no thought, considered to be the most difficult, especially for beginners.

- Contemplation of an object, such as a candle flame, a flower, statue, picture, or a mandala, a symbol representing unity.

- Mental repetition of a sound, which may be a single syllable, such as OM; a mantra, usually a Sanskrit phrase; or a koan, which is an apparently insoluble riddle, such as "What is the sound of a single hand clapping?"

- Detached observation of what is happening without being caught up in or identifying with any reaction to it. The focus is centered on the present moment, and the mind observes itself observing life as it unfolds.

Whatever form of silent meditation is used, it requires nothing more complicated than to sit quietly and enter deeply into one-mindedness. If the mind wanders, the meditator is instructed to bring it gently back to the focus and not allow it to be distracted. In "The Meditative Mind," Daniel Goleman writes that the "key attributes of this state are always the same: loss of sense awareness, one-pointed attention to one object to the exclusion of all other thoughts, and sublimely rapturous feelings."

Okay, I've described different kinds of meditation, but what exactly is it and how does it work? Scientists have come up with several different models that attempt to answer these questions. One model views meditation as a mechanism to reduce stress and anxiety. Another views meditation as nothing more than light sleep, a controlled version of the trance state most people experience as they fall asleep. Another model suggests that meditation is a form of self-hypnosis, although there are others who say that the mind deals with information at different levels in hypnosis than while in a meditative state. For our purposes, the end result is what matters, not the method.

Psychologist Arthur Deikman says, "Although the power of meditation to affect physiological and psychological functions has been substantiated in many different laboratories, we have paid little attention to what the originators have said about its intended purpose and the requirements for its appropriate use. Focusing primarily on the experiences and bodily effects of meditation is like collecting oyster shells and discarding the pearls. Such 'spiritual materialism' inevitably interferes with the real potential of meditation."

Meditation is a procedure, a technology. As such, it facilitates outcomes such as stress reduction and consciousness during sleep. Although these outcomes are a natural part of the biology of the human system and can surface spontaneously without meditation, it clearly increases the likelihood of attaining these outcomes.

What the originators say is that consciousness is the primary reality from which matter and life arose. Through meditation, an individual can more fully experience the pure consciousness that lies at the center of being.

As we enter into these states of consciousness, we are able to move past the stuck spot in our lives, the place where we have remained frozen in our beliefs. We are able to change our beliefs and behaviors in response to one another. This process requires us to extend ourselves, which results in growth.

OTHER INTERNAL TECHNIQUES

The whole process of the evolution of human consciousness rests in the ability to identify oneself as separate from while participating in an ever-expanding involvement with the world. Higher states of consciousness are a natural progression when they are awakened in an individual who has thoroughly completed the development of the basic ego structure. Yet, achieving the merger of self with Self presents a challenge to the ego. Always on guard, the ego rules out the experience of oneness and makes the experience of connectedness difficult.

There is a wide range of inner-oriented techniques other than meditation that focus attention inward toward the source of being, such as lucid dreaming and other dream work, waking imagery and creative visualization, journal keeping, and self-hypnosis. I'll briefly discuss each one; you can obtain other books that go more thoroughly into each subject than I have the space to do here.

Almost one hundred years since the publication of Freud's classic "Interpretation of Dreams," dream work is receiving widespread recognition as a valuable technique for learning more about the self rather than being dismissed as merely phantasms of the sleeping brain. For example, there are professional dream organizations; movies with dream themes are raking in millions; bookstore shelves are filled with dream books, and magazine articles on working with dreams have become almost monthly fare.

During the passionate embrace of altered-state-of-consciousness work in the 1960s, one study paid a young man a full-time salary to record his dreams over the span of a year. He settled into a small mobile home and set out to record his nightly encounters. With some practice, he was recording up to one hundred pages of material a day. What became incredibly clear was that the source of his nightly excursions was the experience of awareness.

A particular form of dreaming, lucid dreaming, offers us a direct link to the experience of pure consciousness. The ultimate self-awareness experience in sleep is knowing you are dreaming while you are dreaming, yet this is but another bridge to even higher levels of consciousness.

Although dreams are the psyche's deepest imagery generating system, we can also benefit through the conscious application of imagery experienced in creative visualization. Jeanne Achterberg, president of the Assocation for Transpersonal Psychology, draws a line from the image to the immune system to support a neurological relationship between the image and the body's maintenance of health. Pointing to the central role of emotions in both imagery and disease, she states, "Verbal messages must undergo translation by the imagery system before they can be understood by the involuntary or autonomic nervous system and related components."

EXTERNAL TECHNIQUES

There are external techniques that help intensify awareness as well. Among these techniques are yoga, sports, games, martial arts, active forms of meditation using chanting, dancing and music, and other physical activities that produce what is popularly referred to as "flow." In every case, the important thing is not the activity itself but the experience of pure consciousness it facilitates. Even mundane activities can access this consciousness, as this story illustrates:

Ram Dass, a.k.a. Richard Alpert, tells of a time he was lecturing to a group of young people about meditation and higher states of consciousness. Both he and the audience were attired in long, flowing robes and requisite beatific smiles. In the midst of this sea of robes and smiles was an elderly woman wearing a brightly flowered housedress, matching hat and sensible shoes. She too often nodded with a knowing smile during his lecture on the beauty of higher states of consciousness. The teacher wondered how it was she apparently identified with what he was saying. She did not appear to "belong" to the audience to whom he was speaking. Afterward, he asked her how she "knew." The elderly lady in the flowered hat leaned over in a conspiratorial fashion and whispered, "I crochet!"

Repetitive activity entrains the brain. A contemporary form of this can be seen in the popularity of Nintendo. While parents grumble about the apparently addictive quality of the game, new research has shown that Nintendo trains hyperactive children to be attentive, which is the major problem in hyperactivity. Mihaly Csikszentmihaly, Professor of Psychology at the University of Chicago, has researched the experience of pure consciousness in daily activities; he calls this "flow", and summarizes his work in his book titled "Flow: The Psychology of Optimal Experience." Some of the activities that produced flow included games, gambling, television viewing, and sex.

In the sports arena, the "runner's high" has been well-known for years; lesser known are the effects on consciousness of other sports. Hans Joachim Stein says of Kyudo, the art of zen archery, that "like any serious practice whose aim is to penetrate beyond appearances to the essence of things and the meaning of life, the Way of the Bow can only be considered to have reached an end with the transmutation of the archer's earthly existence." Even a "non-sport" such as golf, which has been praised by writer John Updike as "the one [sport] wherein the walls between us and the supernatural are rubbed the thinnest," can produce beneficial changes that lead to pure consciousness.

The increasing popularity of martial arts, evidenced by movies such as *The Karate Kid* and even the ubiquitous *Teenage Mutant Ninja Turtles*, emphasizes that the importance of the external form lies in the interior experience.

Psychologist Charles Tart tells the story of Morehei Uyeshiba, master of the Japanese martial art, Aikido, who had witnessed village thugs beating his father:

> I felt that the universe suddenly quaked and that a golden spirit sprang up from the ground, veiled my body and changed it into gold. At the same time my mind and body became light, I was able to understand the whispering of the birds, and was clearly aware of the mind of God, the Creator of this universe. At that moment, I was enlightened: the source of budo is God's love—the spirit of loving protection for all beings. Tears of joy streamed down my cheeks. I understood: Budo is not felling the opponent by force, nor is it a tool to lead the world into destruction. True budo is to accept the spirit of the universe, keep the peace of the world; to take God's love, which correctly produces, protects and cultivates all beings in Nature, and assimilate and utilize it in our own mind and body.

In a world seemingly full of hate and violence, this man was able to deal with disharmony in a spirit of love.

CONCLUSION

Di-no-saur (n.): Any of various prehistoric, extinct, often gigantic reptiles; a person with obsolete ideas, beliefs, attitudes.

We pause on the threshold, hands outstretched to embrace the long-sought missing thing. When the light floods through the open door of our awakened perceptions, what we experience is the shock of recognition. The seeker and the sought after are one.

Standing near a 600-year-old oak tree, I reflected on how it was already old when I was born and will probably be here long after I am gone. Our current lives are not long. Long enough to learn what is required of us, what we need to learn, but not long enough to change much of anything but ourselves.

Many of you are bound by what you feel is a past you never wanted and a future that cannot be. Therein lie frustration, confusion and fear. Dissolution and change frighten you. You want the security of knowing where you are going, how you're going to get there, and what's going to happen to you when you do get there. But you'll never know for certain because life has many possibilities, a few probabilities, and even fewer absolutes. Life is like that. Failure to adapt to these variables in the changing circumstances of life is what leads to extinction.

Negative experiences exact a price from us, as do positive ones. One price of fame and recognition, for example, is the burden of others' expectations. Good fortune will always require more of us than failure ever does. We're living a momentous adventure, the end of an age, and this adventure has its price also. There is always a price for balance to be maintained, which is why every increase, whether personal or worldwide, is met by a decrease somewhere. This adventure is where we earn the currency required to enter the "New Era" predicted by so many. That currency is awareness, and it is acquired at a very high cost. That cost is the release of the old, which is always the price of the new. Few are willing to pay this high price, but the fact that a price must be paid may be the proof that it is worth it.

This New Era will undoubtedly be very different from what is expected. Be willing not to know, not to be sure, and you won't be disappointed or postpone what is to be. Instead of spending valuable energy on theories and fantasies of what the New Era will be, evolve by focusing your attention on the work at hand. Life reveals many secrets to those who wait, watch, and listen. Time always fulfills itself. Stop expecting others to do for you what you need to do for yourself. Look beyond everything you see, then look higher still.

Nothing in nature is clumsy. We are all creatures of our time, the "good guys" **and** the "bad guys." Each body is created for a life particular to its own unique purpose. Do what you were born to do, be what you were born to be. Accept it. Don't be a dinosaur. Drink deeply of life on its terms and you won't become obsolete.

Be willing to release all past beliefs; all gods and

goddesses; avatars and saviors. What worked *then* won't work *now*. What worked for *them* won't work for *you*. Their time is over. This is our time. It is meant for us, for you and for me. Let's move gracefully and lovingly into this brave New Era, unspoiled and free of the past—ALL of it!

> *And after all the journeying, all the pain and joy, we may discover that the Transformation was difficult to grasp, not because it was so far away but because it was so very near. To find the immense world of delight is, in the end, to come home again, where it always was.*
>
> *—George Leonard, "The Transformation"*

ABOUT THE AUTHOR

For eight years, **Michael Misita** has hosted a cable television show called "Michael Misita On ..." The program is broadcast weekly on several Southern California cable systems, and is always a stimulating exploration of human potential. Michael is also a noted speaker, teacher and author on transformational subjects.

Michael often introduces his communications by saying, "I'm not teaching a philosophy, I am simply encouraging you by sharing from my own experience how you can be more present, more aware. How to be open, available, sensitive, vulnerable—one with Life. It's about discovery. What I have to say is of little importance compared to what you gather out of observing yourself. This seeing is not only seeing through the eyes and nerves, but seeing with your heart, with your mind ... seeing completely.

"Unless you cease holding onto the conceptual and burdensome past that enslaves you and come back to the present, you are doomed to continue in the perpetual mechanical dream state from which all life's misery flows. The sooner you become alert, the better. The sooner you become aware and drop out of the trap of accumulated knowledge, the better. Because Life will not wait for you and your theories. It's moving too fast. You are a living 'happening.' You are the adventure. Discover and live this truth now. It happens here and now. In fact, that's the only way it happens ... if you will only allow it."

* * * * *

Anyone desiring to be on Michael's mailing list, or wishing to obtain his TV show for cable-access broadcast in their area, may call him at 213/669-0587, or write to: Michael Misita, P.O. Box 27335, Los Angeles, CA 90027.

FREE SUBSCRIPTION
(Just Send Us Your Receipt Or A Copy of
Your Receipt For This Book)

Master of Life WINNERS is a quarterly magazine sent FREE to all Valley of the Sun book/tape buyers and seminar attendees. We'll be glad to mail you a free sample issue, or if you'll send us your receipt for this book, we'll send the magazine free for a year.

Each issue is approximately 100 pages and contains news, research reports and articles on the subjects of metaphysics, psychic exploration and self-help, in addition to information on all Sutphen Seminars, and over 350 audio and video tapes: Hypnosis, meditation, sleep programming, subliminal programming, silent subliminals, and New Age music. A sampling of some of our audio and video tapes and books will be found on the following pages.

Valley of the Sun Publishing
Box 38, Malibu, CA 90265
Phone: 1-800-421-6603

TRINARY BRAIN/MIND PROGRAMMING

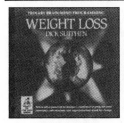

WEIGHT LOSS
CDM01—$14.95

CONFIDENCE &
POSITIVE THINKING
CDM02—$14.95

GOAL COMMITMENT
& SUCCESS
CDM03—$14.95

Each CD contains over 60 minutes of powerful mind-programming, produced with beautiful music and 3-D sound effects.

Programming Content

Track 1: Relaxation—Each CD offers a different peaceful environment to visualize and enjoy as Dick relaxes your body.

Track 2: Mind-Programming Suggestions & Visualizations—Four techniques: 1) Suggestions worded for maximum subconscious acceptance; 2) A mantra technique; 3) "Directed" mental movies; 4) Trigger words.

Track 3: Symbol Therapy—A psychosynthesis visualization technique to focus free-floating psychological energy. The visualizations help to undo past conditioning and establish new energy patterns. Each CD uses 2 to 4 visualizations produced with 3-D sound effects.

Track 4: The Messenger—A visitor provides tips on how to accomplish your goals. The original suggestions are repeated at end.

Track 5: Awakening.

Track 6: Beta-Talk Subconscious Reinforcement—The primary suggestions are rephrased from an "I" perspective, and you are asked to repeat each one.

Each **Trinary Brain/Mind Programming CD Meditation** comes packaged in a standard CD jewel box and offers complete instructions.

.... **$14.95 each**

149

MORE BOOK TITLES

Available Through Your Local Metaphysical Bookseller
Or Directly From Valley of the Sun Publishing

50 SPIRITUALLY POWERFUL MEDITATIONS

By Margaret Rogers

An important addition to every metaphysical library. The book begins with complete meditation instructions that guarantee successful results. Attain advice and find direction through contact with your Higher Mind and living souls in spirit. Meditation is a tool to actualize your potential, achieve greater personal harmony and attain a higher level of awareness. It's easy. It's spiritually powerful. It works. Beautiful full-color cover, 132-page trade-size paperback.

.... B934—$9.98

REINVENTING YOURSELF

By Dick Sutphen

A complete metaphysical self-renewal system. Dick has formulized and added to the trainer techniques he has used so effectively for 16 years in human-potential seminars. With simplified explanations and dialog examples, he provides a unique and extremely powerful system to find your own blocks. Next, you explore the action required to eliminate the problem, followed by the encouragement to create a new reality. Full-color cover, 180-page trade-size paperback.

.... B927—$9.98

YOGA, YOUTH & REINCARNATION

By Jess Stearn

Through the ages, the ancient science of yoga has helped men and women maintain their youth and taught them how to tap their vast reserves of energy. Includes a complete set of do-it-yourself instructions and illustrations. Jess says, "I have managed to remain youthful, optimistic and productive, with as much energy and interest in life as I ever had. I am frequently asked if I have had a face lift. And I say yes, with Yoga." Full-color cover, 336-page trade-size paperback.

.... B935—$9.98

BLAME IT ON YOUR PAST LIVES

By Tara Sutphen

The book started with Tara's column in *Master of Life WINNERS* magazine. **Blame It On Your Past Lives** is a collection of letters and Tara's automatic writing responses showing cause and effect.

The book offers enlightening information about walking a spiritual path. At the end of the book are detailed instructions on how to do automatic writing using Tara's technique. Beautiful full-color cover, 192-page trade-size paperback.

.... B933—$9.98

MORE BOOK TITLES
Available Through Your Local Metaphysical Bookseller
Or Directly From Valley of the Sun Publishing

HEART MAGIC
By Dick Sutphen

Mystical stories about finding love and answers by one of the world's bestselling New Age authors. The tales teach life-changing metaphysical concepts while making you laugh and bringing tears to your eyes. The stories include: *Soulmate Location Service, The Other Lindy, Beneath Sedona, Auric Light, The Walk-In; Those Who Share Our Energy; Guardian Angel; Greater Good; The Chair,* and *The Beginning.* Beautiful full-color cover, 256-page trade-size paperback.
.... **B926—$9.98**

THE SOULMATE PROCESS
By Bob Lancer

A practical book on releasing blocks and directing energy to manifest a soulmate relationship (or transform an existing relationship). It explains what you can do to obtain the love of your life, and guides you through exercises and procedures that engage you as an active participant doing things to help yourself. Beautiful full-color cover, 128-page trade-size paperback. ...... **B928—$9.98**

THE SPIRITUAL PATH GUIDEBOOK
By Dick Sutphen

For twenty years, Sutphen has taught metaphysics, conducted seminars and written some of the all-time bestselling books on the subject. In **The Spiritual Path Guidebook**, he condenses this wisdom down to hundreds of short, life-changing concepts and presents them in this easy-to-assimilate format. 128 page meditation-size paperback with a beautiful full-color cover.
.... **B930—$5.95**

PAST-LIFE THERAPY IN ACTION
By Dick Sutphen & Lauren L.Taylor

Past-life therapy is becoming more commonly accepted, not only by the general population but by the brain/mind professionals as well. No one can deny the life-changing results attainable with these techniques. The authors explore many exciting case histories and show the cause, the effect and the karmic lesson, providing human-potential awareness of how to rise above the undesirable situations. Trade paperback; 144 pages.
.... **B915–$7.95**

Reincarnation For Young People
The Nasty Dragon Who Became a Nice Puppy
By Dick Sutphen

Thirty-two page beautifully illustrated book and audio cassette with 3-D sound effects. Dick has written and illustrated a gentle story that teaches reincarnation to young children (ages 3 to 8). The story follows an animal through three incarnations, communicating the ideas of karma and rebirth very effectively....... **B929—$10.98**

SEDONA:
Psychic Energy Vortexes

One of our most popular titles, now in an updated and expanded version. We've added a new map, the latest information on access to the vortex locations, and lots of new case histories. Sedona is the location of a vortex energy center that enhances all psychic abilities. A fascinating exploration of psychic abilities and the unlimited power of the mind. 228 pages, trade-size paperback.
.... **B922—$9.98**

VIDEO HYPNOSIS® TAPES
Available Through Your Local Metaphysical Bookseller
Or Directly From Valley of the Sun Publishing

Self-change doesn't get any easier or more powerful than this! There is no audio or video tape on the market offering this much programming power. With video, two extra dimensions of brain/mind technology are incorporated, resulting in four times the programming power: Visual hypnosis, as well as the verbal body relaxation and induction, and subliminal programming, which uses suggestions quickly flashed on the screen as well as embedded into the soothing background music. This incredible four-way combination makes these videos the most powerful self-change tapes in the world.

Settle back and turn on the television. You are directed through a soothing mind/body relaxation as you watch visual effects reminiscent of a space odyssey movie. Then, during the main programming content, each tape uses completely different animation effects to turn you inward. At this inward alpha level, suggestions are accepted by your subconscious mind as new beliefs. Beliefs generate thoughts and emotions, which create your experiences. Change your beliefs and you change your life. Thanks to this incredible technology and awareness of how the mind works, change no longer has to be difficult. Each tape is 30 minutes long. **VHS only. $19.95 each.**

• • • • •

VHS103	Lose Weight Now	VHS123	Charisma: Drawing People To You
VHS104	Stop Smoking Forever		
VHS105	Master of Life	VHS124	Stop Punishing Yourself
VHS106	Incredible Self-Confidence	VHS126	Sports Improvement
VHS107	Un-Stress	VHS127	Quick Thinking
VHS108	Ultra-Monetary Success	VHS129	Past-Life Regression
VHS109	Chakra Balance	VHS133	Mind Over Muscles
VHS110	Attracting Love	VHS134	Golf Programming
VHS111	Accelerated Learning	VHS136	Overcoming Addictions
VHS112	Healing Acceleration	VHS138	Physical & Mental Fitness
VHS113	Develop Psychic Ability Now	VHS139	Ultimate Relaxation
VHS114	Intensifying Creative Ability	VHS140	Boost Your Brainpower
VHS116	Incredible Concentration Ability	VHS141	Perfect Weight, Perfect Body
VHS117	Love & Believe in Yourself	VHS146	Sensational Sex
VHS118	Accomplish Your Goals	VHS147	Increase Self-Discipline
VHS119	Positive Thinking	VHS149	Banish Boredom
VHS120	Good Health	VHS150	Reinvent Yourself
VHS122	Channel for the Light	VHS151	Zen Attitude

RX17® AUDIO TAPES
Available Through Your Local Metaphysical Bookseller
Or Directly From Valley of the Sun Publishing

RX17® tapes incorporate state-of-the-art digital recording and the latest brain/mind technology to synchronize both halves of your brain. You are then receptive to new beliefs.

Side A: Alpha Level Programming: Descriptions of a tropical island beach at sunrise are integrated into a body relaxation; ocean waves roll in and out in digital 3-D sound. Subliminal "follow-response" technology lulls you into a soothing alpha level. Next, each tape delivers suggestions that use mind imprinting techniques to help create who and what you want to be!

Side B: Subliminal Programming: Contains 30 minutes of relaxing, digitally recorded stereo music. Each tape uses different music. Subliminal suggestions are synthesized and projected in the same chord and frequency as the music; only your subconscious mind hears. The suggestions are printed on the package. You may also use this side of the tape as **sleep programming.** Simply listen as you go to sleep; it is incredibly powerful. **$12.50 each.**

Dream Solutions
Find Your Answers In Your Dreams

A Dick Sutphen
RX17 Digital-Holophonic™ Audio Cassette
The Most Powerful Brain/Mind Programming Tape In The World

• • • • •

RX101	Powerful Person	RX132	Power & Success
RX102	Attracting Perfect Love	RX134	Charisma
RX103	A Calm & Peaceful Mind	RX135	Do More In Less Time
RX104	The Good Life	RX136	Ultimate Relaxation
RX105	Accelerated Learning	RX145	Forgive & Release
RX106	Dream Solutions	RX146	Overcome Procrastination Now
RX107	Success & Excellence	RX148	Positive Thinking
RX108	Your Last Cigarette	RX149	Eliminate Depression
RX110	Satisfaction & Happiness	RX150	Creative Visualization
RX111	Perfect Weight, Perfect Body	RX152	Sensational Sex
RX112	Sleep Like A Baby	RX153	Letting Go of Guilt
RX115	Create Wealth	RX154	Rising Above Negativity
RX116	Radiant Health	RX155	Stop Punishing Yourself
RX117	Healing Force	RX157	Stress Control
RX118	Right-Brain Solutions	RX158	Eliminate Worry & Fear
RX121	Banish Pain	RX161	Manifest a Miracle in Your Life
RX124	Weight Loss	RX162	Eliminate Eating Disorders
RX126	Concentration Power Plus	RX163	Stop Drinking
RX127	Incredible Self-Confidence	RX164	Stop Drugs
RX128	Intensify Creative Ability	RX166	Increase Self-Discipline
RX131	A Great Memory	RX169	Breath of Life

TARA SUTPHEN AUDIO TAPES
Available Through Your Local Metaphysical Bookseller
Or Directly From Valley of the Sun Publishing

Vision Quest

A beautiful guided meditation to explore psychic solutions and visit your sacred place where you will find peace and higher understanding. You are guided through several explorations until you begin to ask psychic questions. **Side B:** The same beautiful music used on Side A. .... TS201—$9.98

Shaman Journey

A beautiful guided meditation to explore your joys, burdens, goals and new directions. You'll discover life-changing insights and special messages from Higher Mind. **Side B:** The same beautiful music used on Side A.
.... TS202—$9.98

Dream Dance Meditation

A soothing meditation to release the past, explore the present and see a positive vision of your future. **Side B:** The same beautiful music used on Side A. .... TS203—$9.98

Walk of Life

A beautiful guided meditation to explore the unrecognized forces that influence, motivate and restrict your life. Each step of the process helps you to better understand yourself. **Side B:** The same beautiful music used on Side A. .... TS204—$9.98

Automatic Writing

A beautiful guided meditation to explore the powerful process of automatic writing. Your spirit guide is called in, and the technique is clearly explained before you begin automatic writing. **Side B:** The same beautiful music used on Side A...... TS205—$9.98

Spirit Guide Meditation

A beautiful guided meditation to meet your spirit guide and find out about the connection you share. You'll have time to ask questions about your life, loves, goals and spirituality. **Side B:** The same music used on Side A.
.... TS206—$9.98

Akashic Records Meditation

A beautiful guided meditation to learn about your past lives, present loves and earthly purpose. You ascend an ancient stairway to the heavens, where you find a magnificent temple of knowledge. **Side B:** The same beautiful music used on Side A.
.... TS207—$9.98

Amulet Meditation

An enchanting meditation in which you revive an amulet and use it to perceive psychic messages. You will see a positive vision of your future in the clear waters of a fountain. **Side B:** The same beautiful music used on Side A. .... TS208—$9.98

Sea Odyssey Meditation

A wondrous meditation to communicate with dolphins, open your heart chakra and explore your potential. You end this beautiful exploration by sending a telepathic message to humankind. **Side B:** The same beautiful music used on Side A. .... TS209—$9.98

MEDITATIONS ON CD

Available Through Your Local Metaphysical Bookseller
Or Directly From Valley of the Sun Publishing

TEMPLE OF LIGHT

Meditation Journey
By Dick Sutphen

CD format for length and ultra-quality sound: A 65-minute mind-movie meditation in which you become the central character on a journey into the mountains of your mind. Produced with 3-D sound effects, you journey to the Himalayas, and the trek, mountains, and people become real to you.

Travelers along the trail talk to you, ask soul-searching questions, and provide messages the Masters have asked them to relay. Eventually, you reach **The Temple of Light**, where you'll experience a life-changing initiation, and be offered the opportunity to have all your questions answered.

.... **CD777—$14.95**

• • • • •

GATELESS GATE

Meditation Journey
By Dick Sutphen

CD format for length and ultra-quality sound: A 72-minute meditation verging on "virtual reality." You become the central character on a journey of self-discovery.

Produced with beautiful music and incredible 3-D sound effects, you journey to a mountain ashram, where you meet eleven fellow travelers and kindly Brother Joshua, who conducts dharma talks, directs sitting and walking meditations, and one-to-one sessions.

Again and again, you'll be directed to seek awareness about your own life and spiritual quest. Each time you visit the **Gateless Gate**, you can obtain new understanding. .... **CD778—$14.95**